THE CONQUESTS OF ALEXANDER THE GREAT

BY ALISON BEHNKE

TWENTY-FIRST CENTURY BOOKS
MINNEAPOLIS

To Madeleine Fabris-Brown, an inspiring teacher and historian, for introducing me to Alexander in the first place.

Consultant: David Mulroy, University of Wisconsin-Milwaukee

Primary source material in this text is printed over an antique-paper texture.

Front cover: *Alexander is shown at the Battle of Hydapses in India (326 B.C.) in this detail from Charles Le Brun's seventeenth-century painting* Alexander and Porus.

Twenty-First Century Books
A division of Lerner Publishing Group, Inc.
241 First Avenue North
Minneapolis, MN 55401 U.S.A.

Website address: www.lernerbooks.com

Library of Congress Cataloging-in-Publication Data

Behnke, Alison.
The conquests of Alexander the Great / by Alison Behnke.
p. cm. — (Pivotal moments in history)
Includes bibliographical references and index.
ISBN-13: 978–0–8225–5920–7 (lib. bdg. : alk. paper)
ISBN-10: 0–8225–5920–X (lib. bdg. : alk. paper)
1. Alexander, the Great, 356–323 B.C.—Juvenile literature. 2. Greece—History—Macedonian Expansion, 359–323 B.C.—Juvenile literature. 3. Greece—Kings and rulers—Biography—Juvenile literature. 4. Generals—Greece—Biography—Juvenile literature. I. Title.
DF234.B38 2008
938'.07—dc22 2006011824

Manufactured in the United States of America
1 2 3 4 5 6 – DP – 13 12 11 10 09 08

CONTENTS

CHAPTER ONE
GREEK LIFE IN THE AGE OF ALEXANDER

The age of Alexander had the good fortune to produce both many artistic achievements and many men of great talent.

—Plutarch, in his essay "On the Fortune or Virtue of Alexander," ca. A.D. 200

The boy watched as his father's servants and horse handlers struggled with the huge stallion. The boy's father, King Philip II of Macedonia, was considering buying the horse from a traveling merchant. But the beast's muscles strained as it bucked and kicked, and the king was quickly losing interest in such an unmanageable creature. Looking on, Alexander lamented that they were losing a fine animal due to their own lack of skill. When Philip asked his son if he truly believed he could do

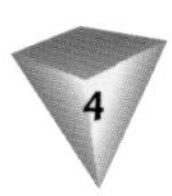

better than his elders, Alexander boldly replied yes. Very well, his father answered—if his boasts proved true, Philip would buy the animal.

The older men laughed scornfully at the youth's arrogance. But their laughter soon turned to amazement. Alexander strode toward the horse. With a perceptive eye, he had noticed that the stallion shied away from his own shadow and those of the handlers. Turning the horse to face the sun, so that he could see neither of their shadows, Alexander petted the animal and spoke softly to him. When the beast was calm, Alexander leapt onto its back, and horse and rider galloped furiously down the plain. When they returned, ancient Greek author Plutarch writes, the men "broke into loud applause, while his father, we are told, actually wept for joy. When Alexander had dismounted he kissed him and said, 'My boy, you must find a kingdom big enough for your ambitions. Macedonia is too small for you.'"

This bust of King Philip II is a copy of an original Greek statue from the fourth century B.C. *Philip reigned as king of Macedonia from 359* B.C. *to 336* B.C.

This tale is one of the most famous stories about Alexander's life (356–323 B.C.) and destiny. It has been retold by many authors, from Alexander's time right up to our own. While it may well have a basis in fact, it has probably been embellished over time. Like any modern-day celebrity, Alexander was the subject of plenty of talk—and, frequently, exaggeration. Nevertheless, the ending of that famous story remains true: Macedonia, as it turned out, *was* too small for Alexander. And that rebellious horse, named Bucephalus, became Alexander's own steed. From this small kingdom northeast of modern Greece, Alexander would ride

Alexander is shown astride his horse Bucephalus in this section from a first-century mosaic found in Pompeii, Italy. The mosaic is often called the Alexander Mosaic.

deep into the vast Persian Empire. Conquering the powerful Asian realm, he became ruler of much of the known world at that period. He was a general revered in his own time for his military genius, using daring and innovative tactics that are still studied in modern times. His powerful blend of confidence, charisma, and vision would attract admirers and win devoted troops, while his ambition and sometimes ruthless drive would also earn him many critics. He brought Greek language and culture to Persia, and exposed the Greeks themselves to new ideas. And his conquests, travels, and deeds became legendary, even before his death at the age of thirty-three. He was born as Alexander III of Macedon. He would die as Alexander the Great.

VOICES FROM THE PAST

When studying ancient Greece, it's important to know that even primary sources reflect only a small segment of the population's experiences. Those people who had the education—and the free time—to write about their lives and times were the most fortunate. Most average Greeks and Macedonians could not read or write at all. In addition, most historical works describing Greece were written by Athenians. Athens was also the cultural and artistic center of Greece, and writers, scholars, and philosophers flocked there. Even Alexander the Great's own childhood tutor, Aristotle, was educated in Athens. As a result, many records have at least some pro-Athens bias.

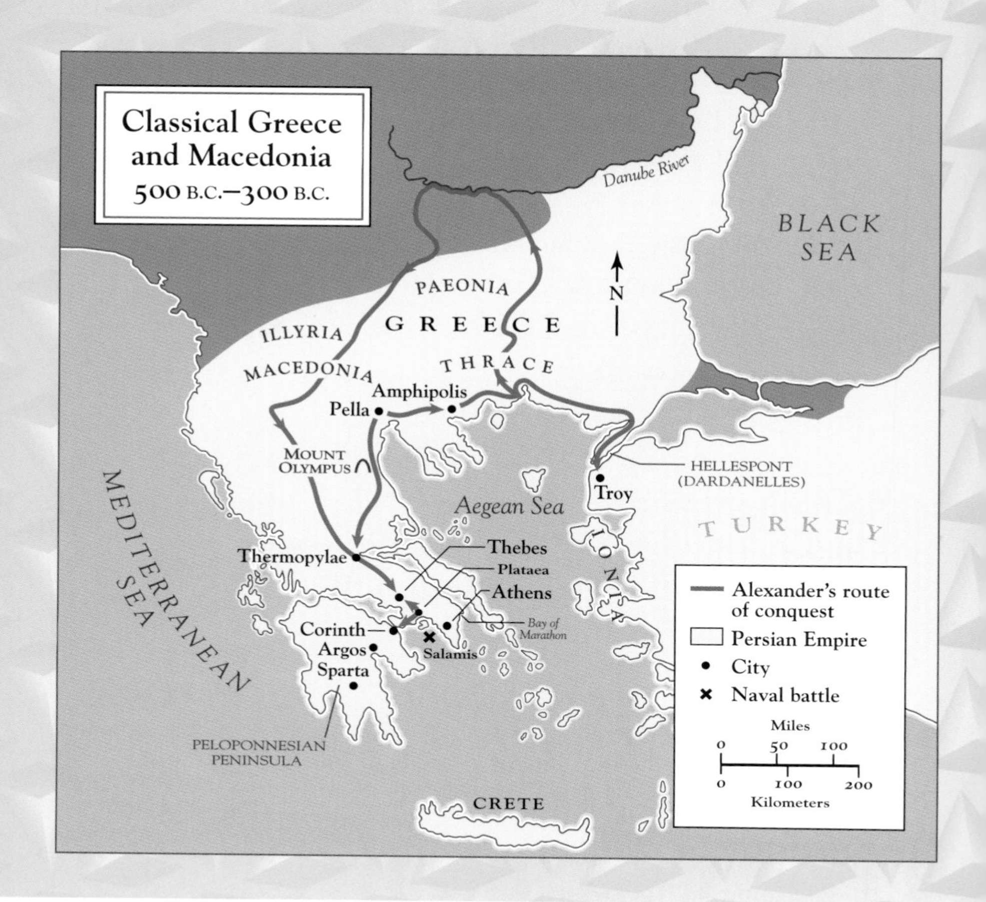

CLASSICAL GREECE

The name "ancient Greece" refers to the areas where the Greek language and its dialects were spoken approximately two thousand to three thousand years ago. Centered on modern-day Greece and Macedonia, the Greek mainland was the core of the ancient Greek world. The southern part of it is the Peloponnesian Peninsula, an arm of land jutting into the Aegean and Mediterranean seas. Scattered along the coastline are dozens of islands, warmed by the Mediterranean sun and washed by the jewel-like blue sea.

Human settlement in this region dates back more than six thousand years, gradually growing, developing, and flourishing. By the time the fourth century B.C. dawned, the Greek world was in the midst of what would later be known as its Classical Period (479–323 B.C.). This era brought prosperity, social and political development, and cultural flowering—if not always peace.

POLIS POLITICS

Greek political life was centered on the city-state, or polis. This governmental and social unit included a city and its surrounding countryside. In the rare cases of Sparta and Athens, this extended up to thousands of square miles. Greek city-states often dealt with one another for trade, military partnerships, or other reasons. But each one was independent, with its own government, economy, and social structure. The Greek language was divided into four or five regional dialects, each of which was used in several city-states.

Not all city-states were created equal. Athens was seen by many as the greatest. Its Acropolis—a hilltop complex of buildings and monuments, including the famous Parthenon temple—remains an impressive sight in modern times. As Athens grew prosperous, it gained a reputation as a center of arts and higher thinking. In 510 B.C., after a period of civil strife, Athens adopted new laws, which are generally considered to have developed the world's first constitutional democracy.

Ancient Athenian democracy was different in many ways from modern democratic systems. Citizens were members of an assembly that met regularly to vote on laws, decisions to go to war, and other issues. Assembly members also elected public officials who helped keep the democratic machinery running smoothly. Another innovation was a justice system that included jurors, allowing people accused of a crime to be judged by fellow citizens.

But there was one major catch in all of this: the only people granted full-fledged citizenship were free adult men whose fathers had been born in Athens. This meant that women, immigrants, and slaves (of whom there were many in ancient Greece) were excluded from the democratic process.

Nevertheless, the system was an important step away from old systems such as monarchy (a government led by a king or queen), oligarchy (a government run by just a few powerful and usually wealthy people), and flat-out tyranny (rule by an often oppressive leader with absolute power). It gave many Athenians their first chance to speak up and play a role in their government. And within a century or two, democracy had spread to some of the city-states beyond Athens.

On the other hand, Sparta—another prominent city-state—never saw much use for the newfangled politics of the people. A dual monarchy with two kings prevailed there.

One citizen differs from another, but the salvation of the community is the common business of them all.

—*from Aristotle's* Politics, 340 B.C.

Sparta focused almost exclusively on achieving military prowess and was famed for the bravery, skill, and ferocity of its warriors. Yet, having poured nearly all of its resources into military pursuits, the city-state developed few other assets. It was primarily agricultural, with little in the way of business or trade. The arts were nearly nonexistent in daily Spartan life—which, organized into a highly disciplined structure of training and athletics, left little time for anything else.

Thebes, Corinth, Argos, and a handful of other city-states also featured prominently in the political, economic, and cultural landscape of ancient Greece. And regardless of size or relative power of their native city-state, residents tended to be fiercely loyal to their own polis.

RELIGION

Greeks and Macedonians shared a set of religious beliefs dating back to 1600 B.C. The Greeks and Macedonians of the 300s B.C., however, lived in a time of changing religious views. Their ancestors had faithfully worshipped a host of deities (gods and goddesses), who made their mythic home on Mount Olympus, a peak in the region of Thessaly. These Olympians were partly used to explain events for which the early Greeks had no scientific explanation. For example, Zeus, the king of the gods, threw thunderbolts when he was angry, while his brother Poseidon controlled the tides and storms of the sea.

These deities were powerful but far from perfect. They often had petty arguments with one another, and they were

I will sing of stately Aphrodite [the goddess of love],
gold-crowned and beautiful. . . . Hail, sweetly-winning,
coy-eyed goddess!

Phoebus [Apollo, the god of light and music], of you even the
swan sings with clear voice to the beating of his wings,
as he alights upon the bank by the eddying river . . . and of
you the sweet-tongued minstrel, holding his high-pitched lyre,
always sings both first and last. . . . And so hail to you, lord!
I seek your favor with my song.

—from the Homeric Hymns, *a collection of early anonymous Greek poems to their gods written between 700 B.C. and 500 B.C.*

fond of meddling in human affairs. A rich oral tradition passed along entertaining stories of their exploits. Trying to figure out the gods' plans, Greeks from craftspeople to kings consulted oracles. These oracles were thought to be in communication with the gods. In response to questions posed by visitors, they passed along cryptic messages that usually left plenty of room for interpretation. Priests and priestesses helped make sense of these replies. Priests also analyzed omens, or signs of the future. It was a big job, as messages from the gods could be hidden in many natural occurrences, such as flocks of birds. To please the deities, people made sacrifices and offerings of animals, food, and wine.

In about the 500s B.C., some Greeks had begun to question the old beliefs. Many sought a deeper spirituality from their religion than the bickering family of Olympians seemed to offer. Many turned to the "mysteries." These secret sects dated back hundreds of years, but gained in popularity in Classical Greece. The secret rites and rituals of these groups were very closely guarded.

At the same time, philosophers such as Socrates and Plato took an entirely different approach to understanding their existence. These thinkers embraced human reason and logic as basic starting points for investigations into the natural world, as well as into deeper questions. In their quest for

Socrates teaches students his philosophies at the Academy in Athens in the fifth century B.C. This engraving is based on an early nineteenth-century painting by Italian artist Bartolommeo Pinelli.

knowledge, Greek philosophers ranged over topics from science and mathematics to government.

Between the new ideas of philosophers and the ancient rituals of the mysteries, many people in Classical Greece explored different belief systems and ways of thinking. But they did not push the old religion aside. The gods and goddesses still inhabited their palace on Mount Olympus and would remain an important part of Greek life for many more generations.

HOUSE AND HOME

Most citizens of the Greek world lived in relatively small, simple homes built of sun-baked clay bricks. These houses were usually painted white to reflect the hot Mediterranean sunshine, and a few small windows were placed high in the walls for light and fresh air. The homes of poorer families generally had only one or two rooms, while richer households sometimes had separate wings for male and female family members. In most homes, rooms were arranged around a central courtyard. This private, open-air space was the focus of family life, and most people spent the bulk of their time outside.

ONLY THE BEST

Elaborate architecture and ornate decoration, along with the best building materials—such as limestone and gleaming white marble—were reserved for the temples and government buildings of ancient Greece.

Foods in ancient Greece tended to be simple, but fresh and flavorful. The warm climate was good for growing a variety of fruits and vegetables, as well as grains such as wheat and barley for making bread. Fish and seafood were abundant in the waters around Greece, but meat was rarely eaten. Herds of goats provided milk for making cheese and yogurt. Olives and olive oil were also an important part of the Greek diet, and wine, made from grapes that flourished in the dry and sunny weather, was served with most meals.

Social class was very important to ancient Greek life. For those at the bottom of the social ladder—which was most of the population—this status was typically hereditary. For example, Greece had many slaves. Many had been captured in war, but others were born into their position. These slaves did a great deal of work, laboring at everything from musical entertainment to mining, and all but the poorest Greek families owned household slaves. And while gaining freedom was sometimes a possibility, most children of slaves were destined to be slaves themselves. In addition, the gap between the richest and the poorest people of Greece was growing in the fourth century. As glorious as Classical Greek civilization was in many ways, life was far from easy for most of the population.

Gender was another major factor in Greek society. Women generally had few rights. They lived under the supervision of a male relative or other guardian from birth to death. They were largely confined to the home, as it was seen as improper for a woman to spend too much time in public. Spartan women were an exception, and they had more freedom than other Greek women. They were expected to be just as tough as their men—in part, so that they could produce strong and healthy children. They were even allowed to take part in certain athletic activities such as boxing.

Greek children followed similar roles as adults, with boys attending school and girls staying at home to learn domestic skills from their mothers. Here again, Sparta was different. Spartan girls went to school for several years—and may have even been put through some of the same hard physical training as boys.

THE FINER THINGS

In between day-to-day duties, the Greeks enjoyed the arts when they could. Live theater was very popular. Audiences crowded the amphitheaters to see comedies by masters such as Aristophanes and tragedies by Aeschylus, Euripides, and Sophocles. Another important art was poetry. The greatest of all Greek poets was Homer, traditionally described as a blind minstrel who lived around 700 B.C. Homer's masterpiece was a pair of epic poems, *The Iliad* and *The Odyssey*, which tell the story of the Trojan War (ca. 1200 B.C.) and its aftermath. All educated Greeks knew some of Homer's words by heart.

Sports were yet another aspect of cultured Greek life. The pinnacle of athletic displays was the famous Olympic Games. The games also had religious meaning, serving as a way to honor the gods and goddesses. Champion athletes were highly respected and held a special and very desirable spot in society.

Sing to me of the man, Muse, the man of twists and turns
driven time and again off course, once he had plundered
the hallowed heights of Troy.
Many cities of men he saw and learned their minds,
many pains he suffered, heartsick on the open sea,
fighting to save his life and bring his comrades home.

—*the opening lines of Homer's* Odyssey

INVASION AND STRIFE

The Classical Period was not all poetry and games, of course. The Greeks also endured years of war, especially the Persian Wars (499–480 B.C.). Persia—a vast Asian empire centered in modern-day Iran—controlled an area called Ionia. This region, lying along the eastern coast of the Aegean Sea in what is now Turkey, included a number of Greek settlements. When these cities revolted against Persian rule in 499, Athens and other city-states joined the fight.

The armies of Persia's King Darius I ended the revolt in Ionia. But Darius didn't stop there. Eager to teach Athens and its allies a lesson, in 490 he ordered the Persian ships to sail to the Bay of Marathon, which was not far from Athens itself.

What followed was an epic battle pitting an estimated ten thousand to twenty thousand Athenian soldiers against close to twice as many Persians. Despite the odds, the Greek

This wall relief from the fifth century B.C. shows Darius on his throne. It was found in the ancient city of Persepolis in modern-day Iran.

forces' exceptional training and some clever battle tactics gave them the edge. They defeated the Persians, and Darius and his men sailed home in defeat.

But the Persians returned in 480 B.C., this time led by Darius's son Xerxes. In a battle at the narrow mountain pass of Thermopylae, the Persians faced the Spartans, who swiftly proved that their reputation as outstanding warriors was well deserved. By the end of the battle's first day, the large Persian force had suffered thousands of casualties, while the Spartans had lost only a small fraction of their troops. But the tide turned when a Greek traitor tipped off the Persians to a route around the pass. The Persians won the battle—though they lost far more men than did the Greeks—and

then marched on Athens, burning the great city to the ground. Most Athenians had already fled, so the death toll was much smaller than it might have been otherwise. As the Greek author Herodotus describes the scene in his *Histories* (440 B.C.), Persian soldiers "managed to scramble up the precipitous face of the [Acropolis]. When the Athenians saw them on the summit, some leapt from the wall to their death, others sought sanctuary in the inner shrine of the temple; but the Persians . . . made straight for the gates, flung them open and slaughtered those in the sanctuary. Having left not one of them alive, they stripped the temple of its treasures and burnt everything on the Acropolis."

The final sea battle of the Persian Wars was just a few weeks later, when the Athenian navy met the powerful Persian fleet at nearby Salamis. Although the Greeks were outnumbered again, they had the advantage in their native waters. To top it off, the Persian troops were exhausted after months of fighting in unfamiliar territory, and many did not know how to swim—leaving them in deep trouble when their ships sank. In a short but bloody battle, the Greeks slaughtered hundreds of Persians, even tracking some of them down on shore. The next year, the Greeks defeated the Persians' large land army at the Battle of Plataea. The wars were over.

The Greek victory over Persia was a great triumph, but bitterness lingered over the burning of Athens. Greeks had little time to dwell on the war, however, as a new conflict loomed in 431 B.C. This time it broke out among the city-states that had so recently united against the Persians. Sparta, frustrated with long Athenian dominance, joined forces with Corinth and other city-states to attack Athens. The resulting Peloponnesian War (431–404 B.C.) ended with the defeat of Athens, making Sparta the most powerful and influential city-state for several decades. Athenian democracy suffered during this period, but democratic ideas and goals lived on in Greece.

FROM THE MOUNTAINS OF MACEDONIA

While the Greeks fought against the Persians and each other, their neighbor to the north had its own designs. Macedonia did not have city-states. It was a kingdom ruled by monarchs who took the throne based on hereditary succession. In 359 B.C., young King Philip II ascended to Macedonia's throne. The new ruler had big plans for his little kingdom. He set to

BARBARIANS IN THE BACKYARD

Some Greeks viewed Macedonians as "barbarians"—inferior foreigners. Greece and Macedonia each had unique traditions and characteristics, and they were sometimes at political and military odds. Yet the Macedonian people spoke a language very closely related to Greek and followed many Greek customs. In fact, Philip himself deeply admired Greek culture. All in all, the affairs, culture, and politics of Greece and Macedonia frequently affected each other.

work updating the Macedonian army, which until then had been disorganized, poorly trained, and insufficiently armed—all in all, an embarrassment to the kingdom. In a few short years, Philip would turn this mess of an army into ancient Europe's best fighting force.

Philip used his new and improved troops to seize the city of Amphipolis, a mining colony that had been fought over for decades. Belonging to Athens, then Sparta, then Athens again, Amphipolis now became Macedonia's, and the gold in its mines gave Philip the means to fund further attacks. Next he set to work conquering the tribal communities of Macedonia's largely wild hills and mountains. These peoples had long been seen as a threat to any stable, centralized Macedonian power. Once this goal was accomplished, Philip looked beyond his own borders. And so, within a decade of taking power, Philip began expanding Macedonian power in all directions—including southward, into Greece.

A LAND ON THE VERGE OF CHANGE

The advancements, conflicts, and alliances that took place between the 500s and 300s B.C. laid the groundwork for much of Greek life and society during the late Classical Age. It was a time of often fierce competition among the Greek city-states—but also of unprecedented Greek unity to fight the Persians, against whom hostility, resentment, and suspicion still lingered. For Macedonia, it was a time of swift growth. And it was a time of changing ideas among Greek peoples about the world in which they lived. It was into this age that Alexander was born.

CHAPTER TWO
"LOFTY AMBITIONS"

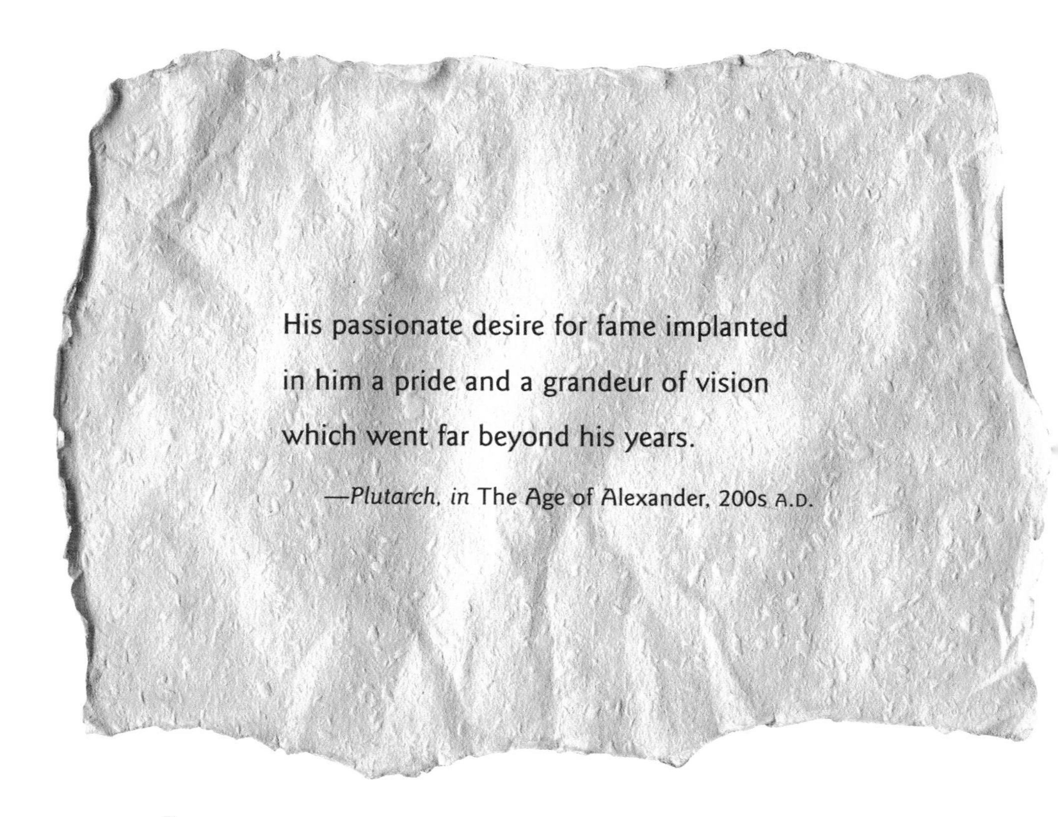

His passionate desire for fame implanted in him a pride and a grandeur of vision which went far beyond his years.

—*Plutarch, in* The Age of Alexander, 200s A.D.

In midsummer 356 B.C., a young Macedonian couple welcomed their first son into the world. King Philip II and his queen, Olympias, named the child Alexander III of Macedon. This newborn infant was the heir to a kingdom gaining in size and strength.

The price of the kingdom's growth was long absences for Philip, who spent many months at a time away at battle, far from his wife and son. Philip's time was also occupied with

This work by a sixteenth-century European artist depicts Alexander's birth, using the style typical of the artist's era.

friendlier visits. The king was a masterful diplomat and made nearly as many strides through negotiating and forging strong relationships as he did through warfare. He would eventually form and lead the League of Corinth, an alliance among Macedonia and most of the Greek city-states. This compact promised peace and cooperation among its members. Still, Philip was by no means timid in battle. During a siege in 354 B.C., he lost his right eye to an enemy's arrow.

King Philip made certain that, even in his absence, his son's days would not be empty. At about the age of thirteen, Alexander began to study under the tutorship of Aristotle, a respected Greek philosopher who had once been Plato's student. Alexander grew fond of his brilliant teacher and gained from him a lifelong love of Greek culture. He also came to value philosophy, medicine, and all pursuits of knowledge and understanding. It was Aristotle, too, who gave Alexander an appreciation for the poet Homer. A copy of *The Iliad* with Aristotle's handwritten notes would become one of Alexander's most treasured possessions.

Alexander also spent time with his friend, Hephaestion. About the same age as Alexander, Hephaestion was a member of Macedonia's noble class. The two probably met while Hephaestion was being educated at Philip's court—possibly even as another student of Aristotle's. The two became close friends.

In the ancient Greek world, where women usually stayed in the home, men and women almost never mingled in public. As a result, men spent most of their time with other men, and it was common for young male friends to have romantic relationships with one another. These romances generally ended when one or the other partner reached adulthood—particularly when one of them got married. However, this was not always the case. Alexander's friend Hephaestion was probably also a romantic companion. But their relationship did not end at adulthood, and they remained devoted friends for their entire lives.

A KING IN TRAINING

While Alexander might sometimes have wished for more time with his father, Philip's absences gave the young prince plenty of chances to prove himself. During one of the king's trips, Plutarch recounts, several foreign ambassadors arrived at the royal court. "Alexander received them . . . and quite won them over, not only by the friendliness of his manner, but also because he did not trouble them with any childish or trivial inquiries. . . . The ambassadors were filled with admiration. They came away convinced that Philip's celebrated astuteness was as nothing compared to the adventurous spirit and lofty ambitions of his son."

During another of Philip's absences, sixteen-year-old Alexander found himself temporarily in charge of the entire kingdom. He made the most of the opportunity, even putting down a revolt in the northeastern part of the country. Later, in about 338 B.C., Philip even brought his teenage son into the field with him. In the Battle of Chaeronea, waged against Athenian and Theban forces, the king gave Alexander command of part of the Macedonian force. As Diodorus would later write in his *Histories*, Alexander was "young in age but noted for his valour and swiftness of action." Already, he had shown himself to be skilled in warfare. He also revealed a wide streak of ambition, as he was "yielding to none in will to win."

Despite the prince's many fine qualities, his right to his father's throne fell into dispute in about 337 B.C., when Philip left Olympias for a second wife named Cleopatra (not the famous queen of Egypt, who lived at a later time). Unlike Olympias, who was from the Greek region of Epirus, Cleopatra was of pure Macedonian blood. Should Philip and his new bride have a child together, the heir could pose a serious threat to Alexander's succession.

Meanwhile, however, Philip was planning an expedition into Asia. He mapped out strategies and negotiated with his Greek allies. Billing the expedition partly as revenge against Persia for the destruction of Athens during the Persian Wars, he won approval of his plan from the League of Corinth. To be sure that he also had the support of the gods, he consulted oracles and watched for omens. All developments seemed promising, and Philip was on the verge of leaving in 336 B.C. That same year, he and Cleopatra did, indeed, have a son.

Then, just days after the birth of Alexander's half-brother, Philip was stabbed to death. His assassin's identity remains a mystery. Suspects included a bodyguard or a former romantic partner. Even Alexander and Olympias came under suspicion. But Alexander wasted little time fretting about the charges against him—or even, for that matter, mourning his father. He saw to the details of Philip's funeral, arranging a state function with all the traditional rites. But there was no time to dawdle. Too much had to be done.

PREPARATIONS BEGIN

Philip's assassination could have cut short the dream of Macedonian conquests in Asia. But Alexander, now twenty years old, had no intention of letting that bold ambition die—and no intention of letting anyone but himself achieve it. He quickly called upon the support of the army, whose trust and admiration he had won when he had served with them under Philip's command.

However, Macedonia's army alone would not be enough to march against Persia. Alexander looked next to the city-states of Greece. As members of the League of Corinth, they had pledged their troops to the cause of any other league member. But not all of the Greeks were eager to hand the fates of their armies over to a boy barely out of his teens. Some had not been pleased with Philip's expanding power to begin with—particularly the proud people of Athens—and hoped to seize this change of ruler as an opportunity to stem Macedonian growth. The threat of revolt seemed to hang in the air.

This bust of Alexander is a copy of a statue made during Alexander's lifetime by Lysippus, the most famous sculptor of the time.

Moving to defuse the danger, Alexander traveled to Corinth for face-to-face negotiations. He urged the rebellious leaders to change their minds. Speaking eloquently, Alexander proved to have some of his father's talent for persuasive argument. At the same time, he did not hesitate to use intimidation to achieve his goals. He did more than hint at his willingness to use force, arriving at Corinth backed by troops in battle gear. Just to make sure he got his point across, he ordered the execution of several enemies who were opposed to his rule.

In the end, this combination of tactics proved successful, and Alexander ranged the forces of Greece behind him. As Diodorus writes, "for all the problems and fears that beset his kingdom on every side, Alexander, who had only just reached manhood, brought everything into order impressively and swiftly. Some he won by persuasion and diplomacy, others he frightened into keeping the peace, but some had to be mastered by force and so reduced to submission."

TYING UP LOOSE ENDS

Now the commander of more than thirty thousand men, Alexander was nearly ready to carry out his father's mission. But before he ventured into Asia, he had to face a problem that had plagued Philip, too. Many of the peoples who lived in the wilderness of Macedonia and its border regions remained rebellious. As a result, they still presented a possible threat to the rule of the Macedonian king—especially one who intended to travel thousands of miles from home.

With these concerns in mind, Alexander led troops northeastward against the Triballians, and beyond to the shores of the Danube River. The well-trained and heavily armed Macedonian forces quickly crushed those opponents who chose to fight, while some leaders surrendered without doing battle. Alexander moved on to the west, where challenges existed from tribesmen in Greek areas such as Illyria, but here, too, the resistance was short-lived.

A bigger problem lay on the horizon. The city-state of Thebes had reconsidered its loyalty to Macedonia and had risen up against Alexander. Several other city-states, including Athens, tentatively agreed to support Thebes in its rebellion. Alexander hesitated at first to attack. He wished to avoid delaying his departure for Asia and hoped that the Thebans might yet come to their senses and refrain from fighting the huge Macedonian army. But Alexander soon saw that the threat from Thebes could not be ignored. Defeating the Thebans decisively would, if nothing else, give him the chance to make an example of them. That example, hopefully, would prevent similar uprisings in other city-states.

In early fall 335 B.C., Alexander's men—joined by some Greek soldiers from anti-Theban areas—laid siege to Thebes. The battle that followed was terrifying. The Macedonian forces eventually broke through the city's defenses, fighting in close quarters against the proud Thebans. In the chaotic and bloody struggle, more than six thousand Thebans were killed, with at least thirty thousand more captured. In contrast, only about five hundred Macedonians lost their lives. As Arrian describes it, the Macedonian and Greek forces "in the lust of battle, indiscriminately slaughtered the Thebans, who no longer put up any organized resistance. They burst into houses and killed the occupants; others they cut down even as they attempted to . . . fight; others, again, even as they clung to temple altars, sparing neither women nor children."

The lesson had been made clear. Alexander was now unquestionably the master of Greece and Macedonia. He was twenty-one years old.

THE ARMY OF ALEXANDER

In the spring of 334 B.C., Alexander and his army departed for Asia. He put his father's trusted official Antipater in charge of the kingdom while he was gone.

The Macedonian army that Philip had created was a well-oiled machine with many interlocking parts all working in harmony. It was divided into two sections: the Royal Army and the Territorial Army. The Royal Army was made up of the Royal Companion Cavalry and the Royal Hypaspists. Until Philip's day, most Greek armies hadn't used cavalry (horse-mounted soldiers) very much, relying

BY THE NUMBERS

According to the ancient Roman historian Marcus Junianus Justinus (usually simply called Justin), the size of the army that accompanied Alexander into Asia was 32,000 foot soldiers and 4,500 cavalrymen. Diodorus agrees with these figures, while Arrian estimates that 30,000 infantry and 5,000 cavalry would have been the upper limits of the army's strength. Plutarch provides the widest range: 30,000 to 43,000 in the infantry and 4,000 to 5,000 cavalry. Modern historians estimate a total of about 43,000 infantry and 6,000 cavalry.

mainly on infantry (foot soldiers) to fight their wars. But by the time Alexander took command of the Macedonian force, the cavalry was an integral part of the system. The Companion (*hetairoi*) Cavalry included many Macedonian noblemen. Its members carried heavy weapons such as spears and swords. The most elite group within the Companions was the Royal Horse-Guards, who served as bodyguards for Alexander, as well as often leading charges into battle. A light cavalry (*prodromoi*) assisted the Companion Cavalry, carrying javelins and lightweight spears.

As for the Royal Hypaspists, they were infantrymen. Hypaspists ("shield carriers") fought in a hit-and-run style. But beyond that, it isn't known for sure how they were armed or even what their precise purpose in battle was.

The remainder of Alexander's army was called the Territorial Army. Most of these troops were members of the infantry. The heart of that infantry was one of the most innovative and powerful weapons in the Macedonian army's arsenal: the phalanx.

An old idea that had been improved by Philip, the formation packed soldiers tightly together in a rectangular shape, usually in columns of eight or sixteen men each. One of the secrets of the phalangites (infantrymen who made up the phalanx) was their enormous discipline. They spent long hours fine-tuning their moves with complex practice drills, enabling them to outmaneuver less-skilled foes in battle. Another potent defense was their weaponry. Every man in the phalanx carried a *sarissa*—a double-pointed pike 10 to 20 feet (3 to 6 meters) long. This formidable weapon, said to have been invented by Philip, was held straight forward or angled

A Macedonian phalanx stands in formation holding sarissas. The phalanx was a key part of Philip's and Alexander's armies.

upward, depending on the soldier's position in the phalanx. The phalanx shape and the sarissas together made for a very spiky group, and the combination was so effective that few enemies could get past the sarissas to engage the infantrymen in hand-to-hand combat. As a result, the phalangites generally needed only light armor and small shields, allowing them to move quickly. In addition, the upward-pointing sarissas served as protection from arrows and other airborne weapons.

In addition to the broad categories of cavalry and infantry, the army contained a variety of specialists. Many of these units were made up not of Macedonians but of soldiers from Macedonia's Greek allies. For example, the Thessalians provided a force of aggressive heavy cavalrymen, sometimes known as "shock" troops, meant to inflict quick and heavy casualties on the enemy. Thracians, Illyrians, and Paeonians contributed additional light cavalry and infantry, including a highly skilled force lightly armed with javelins. A unit of Macedonian archers (soldiers armed with bows and arrows) was joined by a second group of archers from the Greek island of Crete. A force of scouts, who rode ahead of the army to gather information, was another valuable element of the Macedonian force.

BEYOND FIGHTERS

An ancient army never traveled light, and Alexander's force was no exception. Bringing up the rear behind the main body of the troops was a baggage train. This vital source of supplies carried stores of food, housing in the form of tents, and other necessities. Servants, cooks, and doctors tended to the troops.

Alexander also brought with him experts on many subjects—some more strictly practical than others. Directly related to the operation of the army, for example, were engineers who designed weapons such as catapults. Additional travelers with the Macedonian force included scientists, enlisted to record observations on the geography, topography, plants, animals, climate, and cultures of each new land that the army traveled through. Philosophers tended to more spiritual needs, sometimes helping interpret omens for the king. One of these philosophers was Callisthenes—a relative of Aristotle—who did double duty as Alexander's official historian.

Along with Alexander, a number of officers led the army. They included Parmenio, who had fought with Philip; Philotas, son of Parmenio and a skilled military leader in his own right; Craterus, a very talented commander; and Alexander's childhood friend Hephaestion. Although Hephaestion was not, according to most historical sources, an outstanding military officer, he remained "by far the dearest of all the king's friends," as Rufus records. He was also a trusted confidant. "He had been brought up with Alexander and shared all his secrets. No other person was privileged to advise the king as candidly as he did, and yet he exercised that privilege in such a way that it seemed granted by Alexander rather than claimed by Hephaestion."

This relief sculpture from Salonica, Greece, depicts Alexander's friend Hephaestion.

ACROSS THE HELLESPONT

Ancient Greek and Macedonian ideas about the world's geography were, in many cases, inaccurate. They divided the earth into three main regions: Europe (stretching roughly from

Spain to Albania), Libya (North Africa), and Asia (roughly the Persian Empire, plus the Arabian Peninsula). These territories were surrounded, they believed, by the Great Ocean—a body of water that encircled the entire inhabited world.

The official crossing from Europe into Asia is marked by the Hellespont. This strait (a narrow waterway connecting two larger bodies of water) lies east of Greece, in modern-day Turkey. It connects the Aegean and Black seas. Crossing the Hellespont was, in ancient days, highly symbolic, and Alexander marked the occasion with appropriate drama. Diodorus writes, "Alexander advanced with his army to the Hellespont . . . where he flung his spear from the ship and fixed it in the ground, and then leapt ashore himself the first of the Macedonians, signifying that he received Asia from the gods as a spear-won prize."

Not far from the Asian side of the Hellespont was Troy, the site of the ancient Trojan War that Homer had described in *The Iliad*. Alexander was eager to reach Persia. But he could not pass by the revered battlegrounds described by Homer without pausing to pay his respects to the heroes and conquerors who had gone before him. The army stopped at Troy, where Alexander visited the tomb of Achilles, the greatest Greek warrior of the Trojan War, while Hephaestion stopped at the tomb of Patroclus, another warrior and Achilles' dearest friend. Alexander—who had carried along his beloved copy of *The Iliad* and slept with it under his pillow—may have seen himself as a worthy successor of Achilles. He once commented that Achilles had been fortunate to have a poet such as Homer to record his deeds. Soon enough Alexander would move on from Troy to seek his own glory.

CHAPTER THREE
TO BATTLE

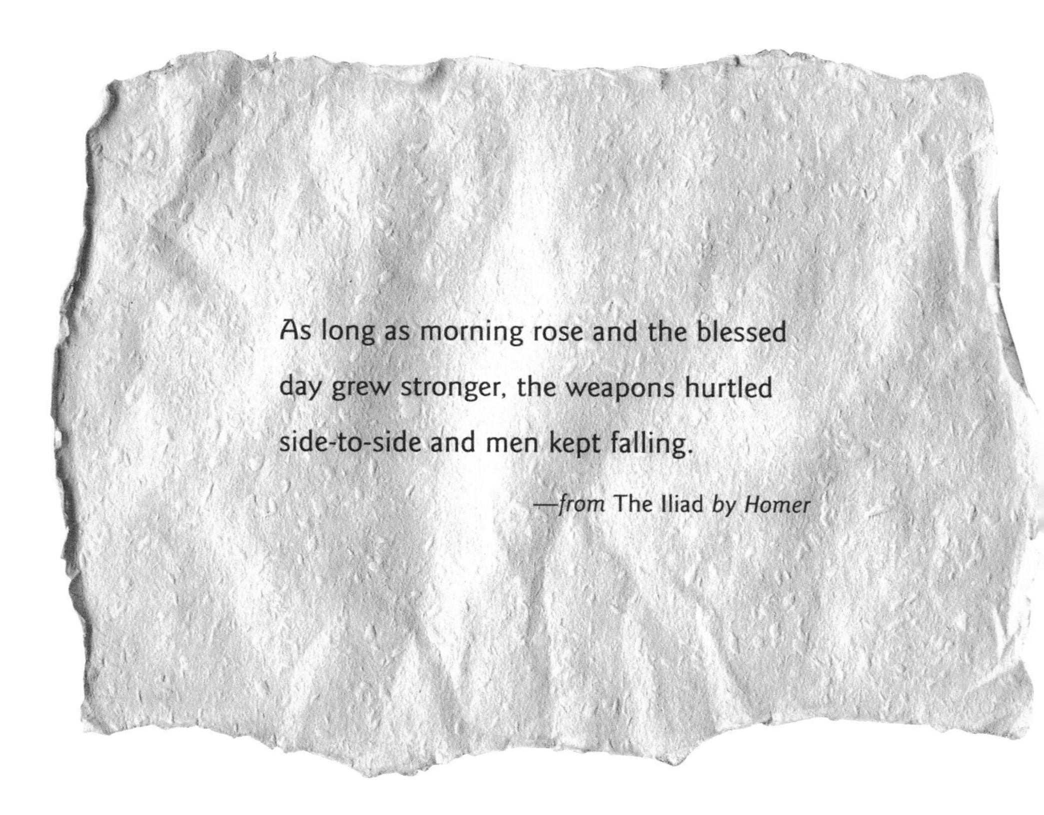

As long as morning rose and the blessed
day grew stronger, the weapons hurtled
side-to-side and men kept falling.

—*from* The Iliad *by Homer*

Under the command of King Darius III, Persia's army was made up of men from across the empire. Each Persian province pledged a certain number of troops, based on its population and prosperity. These forces were organized into *baivaraba* (called myriads by the Greeks)—groups of ten thousand soldiers—and baivaraba were subdivided into thousand-man units called *hazaraba* (*chiliarchies* in Greek). The army had the standard components of heavy and light infantry and cavalry, but compared to the Macedonian army, a greater proportion of the Persian force is believed to have been cavalry. Persian horsemen were well-regarded for their skill. In addition, the steeds of the Persian cavalry were of different breeds from across the vast empire, and some were renowned for their strength and size.

Persian weapons included short swords, bows and arrows, and battle-axes. Infantrymen often carried spears, while the Persian cavalry was generally armed with shorter, lighter javelins instead. Most soldiers carried shields made of wicker and leather and wore only light armor. Like Alexander's army, the Persians also had

This fourth-century B.C. wall relief from Susa, Iran, shows a Persian warrior who served as part of the king's bodyguard.

divisions of specialists, such as a skilled group of archers. A unit of "slingers" used slingshots to launch stone or metal projectiles at the enemy, while a smaller number of troops rode camels or fought from horse-drawn chariots.

The Persian army's most elite soldiers were known as the Athanatoi, or Immortals. This name is thought to refer to the fact that, whenever an Immortal fell in battle, he was swiftly replaced. Due to this practice, the force had a constant strength of ten thousand soldiers. But only men of great physical strength, courage, and overall excellence were chosen to fight in the Immortals. They carried spears approximately 7 feet (2 m) long, with counterweights of silver or gold depending on the soldier's rank.

THE BENEFITS OF BRAVERY

Being an Immortal brought a soldier great honor and social status. But it also won him more tangible rewards—such as more impressive uniforms and tastier meals than those of the rest of the Persian army. Herodotus writes, "Of all the troops in the army the [Immortals] were not only the best but also the most magnificently equipped . . . every man glittered with the gold which he carried about his person in unlimited quantity. They were accompanied, moreover, by covered carriages containing their women and servants, all elaborately fitted out. Special food, separate from that of the rest of the army, was brought along for them on camels and mules."

In the 300s, a growing number of infantrymen in the Persian army were actually mercenaries (hired soldiers) from Greece. With growing unrest in the empire, Persia needed the soldiers—and the soldiers needed the work. In addition, some mercenaries hoped that by fighting against Alexander as he advanced into Persia, they might thwart both that invasion and his rule over Greek territories.

Mercenaries and Persians alike would soon get their chance to test their strength against the army of Macedonia.

Persian messengers reported to Darius that Alexander was on his way. In May or June of 334 B.C., as Macedonian troops marched toward the western bank of the Granicus River (in western Turkey), the Persian army was waiting on the other side.

THE STRUGGLE BEGINS

According to the ancient sources, the Persian troops at Granicus numbered anywhere between thirty-two thousand and six hundred thousand. Modern scholars widely believe that the upper end of this vast range was an exaggeration, probably put forth by authors eager to make the Macedonian army's achievements appear most impressive. A more likely maximum figure is closer to fifty thousand, and, in all probability, the Persian and Macedonian armies were fairly close in size. However, in keeping with its overall makeup, the Persian force at Granicus almost definitely had a much greater proportion of cavalry than foot soldiers.

As Alexander and the army approached the river, his scouts rode ahead to survey the scene. Galloping back to the troops, they reported that the Persians were ranged defensively on the opposite bank of the Granicus—clearly intending to prevent the Macedonians from crossing. Upon hearing this intelligence, Alexander's experienced general Parmenio recommended delaying any attack in the hopes that the Persians might pull back from the river's edge overnight.

Diodorus states that Alexander did wait until dawn of the following day to attack. But according to Arrian and Plutarch, Alexander was in no mood to be dissuaded from carrying out his plan: a quick and decisive victory, establishing in no uncertain terms the threat that Macedonia posed to the Persian Empire. He is said to have replied, "Yes, Parmenio, but I should be ashamed of myself if a little trickle of water like this . . . were too much for us to cross." These were bold words, considering the fact that the Granicus was more than 50 feet (15 m) wide, with a swift current.

In any case, the battle began with the two armies facing each other across the water. Alexander had placed Parmenio in charge of the army's left wing, consisting mainly of cavalry. The king himself led the right wing, made up of the Companion Cavalry, plus units of archers and Agrianians (javeliners). Alexander and Parmenio each commanded part of the sturdy phalanx, which was positioned firmly in the middle of the Macedonian line, along with hypaspists. Other officials led the individual units.

The Macedonians, led by cavalry, plunged into the water and headed for the Persians' left wing. Javelins and arrows rained down upon them as they crossed the Granicus and struggled up the opposite bank, where they met the Persian cavalry and began hand-to-hand fighting. With firm footing

There was a profound hush as both armies stood for a while motionless on the brink of the river, as if in awe of what was to come.

—*from Arrian's* Campaigns of Alexander, ca. A.D. 150

and a greater height, the Persian horsemen had a decided advantage, and the first lines of the Macedonians began to fall.

At this point, with the foe's attention focused on its left flank, Alexander led the Companions in a charge against the center of the Persian troops, driving the heavy Macedonian cavalry near the middle of the enemy line. Alexander threw himself into the thick of the battle. Easily spotted in his royal armor and the brilliant white plume on his helmet, he made a highly sought-after target. As Persian troops began focusing on this tempting prize, additional units of Macedonian cavalry as well as the phalanx streamed across the river.

The battle intensified around Alexander, who fought back fiercely. At one point, a Persian soldier struck Alexander's helmet with his sword. Recovering from the blow, Alexander continued to fight, but another Persian readied himself with a battle-axe for a second blow to the king's damaged helmet. Before the axe could fall, however, the Macedonian officer Cleitus used his own sword to slice off the attacker's arm—axe and all. Alexander was wounded, but alive.

As the struggle raged on, the tables began to turn in the Macedonians' favor. It soon became clear that Alexander's men were better fighters in close-quarters combat. Although the thin Persian shields offered good protection against arrows, they proved far less effective against the powerful Macedonian sarissas. Finally the Persian line disintegrated. As the cavalry retreated in chaos, it exposed the ranks of the infantry. Made up of Greek mercenaries, this force had been massed behind the mounted troops. These men stood their ground, asking Alexander for mercy in exchange for their service. But Alexander's attitude toward mercenaries was harsh—he saw them as nothing less than traitors to Greece. He ordered his troops to surround the mercenaries, and a brutal assault followed that left many of the mercenaries dead. The remainder became prisoners.

Like estimates of original troop strength, casualties reported in the ancient sources usually overstate the number of enemy soldiers killed, while underestimating Macedonian losses. However, at least one thousand Persian cavalry were probably killed at the Granicus, along with several thousand foot soldiers. Thousands more were wounded or taken prisoner. As was the custom in ancient warfare, the Greek and Persian commanders alike had joined their men in the thick of the battle, risking their own lives along with those of their troops. Losses among the Persian leaders—who were

This painting depicts Alexander's victory over the Persians at the Granicus River. It is by seventeenth-century French artist Charles LeBrun.

frequently members of the empire's nobility—were high at the Battle of the Granicus. King Darius, however, had remained safely distant from the conflict.

The Macedonians, in contrast, lost fewer than two hundred men—including, it was reported, twenty-five Companions. Alexander ordered Lysippus to make statues of the fallen to commemorate their bravery. Alexander also sent spoils of the battle, such as the shields of prisoners, back home. In this shipment he included some treasures specifically for his mother, Olympias.

GAINING GROUND

This first battle served, as Alexander had hoped, to intimidate some of the region's leaders. Having heard of the loss at Granicus, the commander Mithrines surrendered his city of Sardis without contest, and many of his neighbors in Ionia followed suit. As Alexander established his control of the area, he began disassembling the systems of rule there and establishing democracies.

As a hereditary king himself, Alexander probably was not democracy's biggest booster. However, the former student of Aristotle loved Greek culture and was happy to spread it through various channels—including government. He also recognized democracy's value as a tool—a tool, ironically, to cement his own rule. A large number of Ionian cities had been Greek settlements before being seized by Persia. But Persian rulers had backed regional oligarchies, thus making people in these Ionian territories hunger for the greater freedom of democracy. Therefore, by publicly supporting democratic systems, Alexander cast himself in the best possible light—that of a liberator rather than a conqueror.

However, some cities in the area still put up resistance against Alexander. One such holdout was Halicarnassus (called Bodrum in modern times)—a strategically important prize. Defended by Memnon, a Greek mercenary who had become one of Darius's principal generals, the city was the capital of the region of Caria. It was also Persia's main naval outpost on the Aegean Sea. In August 334 B.C., the Macedonian army set up camp outside the city.

Alexander and his men anticipated a long—and probably costly—struggle for Halicarnassus. The city was situated in a strong defensive position, with the sea at its back. In addition, it was guarded by sturdy walls and well-armed troops—not to mention the powerful Persian navy, which had warships waiting in the harbor. Should the situation become too dangerous, the Persians could simply evacuate the town by sea.

Alexander launched a series of attacks against the walls, sending cavalry, infantry, archers, and other troops in various assaults. All failed, however, leaving Alexander to attempt a different approach. In order to move the Macedonian siege engines within reach of the walls, his workers first had to fill in part of a deep trench that surrounded the city's landward side. Even when this task had been accomplished, the city's strong walls held up against everything the Macedonians hurled at them. To make matters worse, the Halicarnassians were hardly sitting quietly inside while their city was being attacked. They fiercely counterattacked Alexander's men and set fire to the siege engines.

LAYING SIEGE

Alexander's army traveled with a valuable set of weapons called siege engines. The purpose of these tools was to break through or overcome barriers such as city walls or other fortifications. Macedonian siege engines included battering rams, catapults, and similar heavy weapons.

But after several months, gradual Macedonian progress at breaking through the city's defenses paid off. The siege came to an end with one last, fierce battle. Diodorus reports, "As violent shouts arose at the same time on both sides and the trumpets sounded the attack, a terrific contest ensued because of the valour of the contestants and their consummate fighting spirit." Finally, Alexander's men prevailed—only to enter the town and find that Memnon and his military leaders had already left. After a long, exhausting siege—and the loss of several dozen men—the weary Macedonian troops had won, but it was an empty and painful victory.

With winter drawing near, Alexander led his troops eastward into Lycia (a region along the northeastern shore of the Mediterranean). Turning to the north, they marched toward Phrygia and Cappadocia in modern Turkey. All along this route, the Macedonians fought minor battles, subduing the surrounding areas. In early spring 333 B.C., they reached Gordium, Phrygia's ancient capital.

Alexander had heard of an ancient story of the Phrygians that centered on a wagon in the center of Gordium. According to the tales, the wagon had brought to the realm a leader who ended years of strife. Attached to the wagon was a yoke held in place by a thick cord. The cord was twisted in such a complicated way that neither of its ends could be seen, and the resulting puzzle was called the Gordian Knot. Whoever could undo this knot, it was said, would be the ruler of Asia. Eager to claim that title, Alexander undertook the challenge. What happened next is reported in different ways by the ancient writers. Arrian acknowledges the confusion, saying, "some say that Alexander cut the knot with a stroke of his sword . . . but Aristobulus thinks that he took out the pin . . . which was driven right through the shaft of the wagon and held the knot together." Whatever his method, when Alexander left Gordium, the knot was undone.

Meanwhile, Persian troops continued to threaten the western edges of Alexander's territory. Memnon led several attacks in the Aegean, claiming several islands, and even laid plans for an invasion of Greece. But in August, Memnon died—depriving Darius of a brilliant commander and ridding Alexander of a troublesome foe.

Soon afterward, Darius himself left his palace at Susa and began moving an army northeastward to confront Alexander. Hearing news of this advance from his scouts, Alexander was eager to meet his Persian counterpart in a heroic battle.

In the fall, Alexander left Gordium and continued on to the southeast, passing through the Cappadocia region and into Cilicia. Believing that Darius was approaching from the southeast, Alexander continued on toward Syria. But unbeknownst to the Macedonians, Darius, moving swiftly, was actually leading his army to the north and circling back in the rear of Alexander's forces.

Thus, in the late fall of 333, Alexander was unpleasantly surprised to find that Darius was behind him. Not only did this development mean that the Persians were in territory that the Macedonians had already seized, but it meant that Alexander's access to supplies was blocked. As the Persians advanced southward, Alexander had little choice but to wheel his army around and fight Darius earlier than planned. Preparing for battle, he took up a position near the city of Issus in southern Turkey.

A TIGHT SPOT

As the armies of Darius and Alexander readied for battle, there was no question that this time, the Persian forces were truly superior in numbers. An estimated one hundred thousand troops or more stood ready to fight for the empire versus thirty thousand to fifty thousand Macedonians and Greeks. And, perhaps having learned from the Granicus, Darius had included many more infantrymen in his battle ranks.

Despite being caught off-guard by Darius's unexpected route and being badly outnumbered, Alexander's men soon found that the setting of the battle worked to their advantage. Bounded by the Mediterranean Sea to the west and mountains to the east, the armies met on a narrow, marshy field. This limited area forced Darius to divide his troops into small units, rather than attacking in one overwhelming mass. As a result, the huge numerical advantage that the Persians would have had on an open plain was lost.

As usual, Alexander took charge of the right wing and placed Parmenio on the left, with the phalanx at the core of the line. Light infantry, cavalry, and archers manned the wings. Facing the Macedonian army, Darius led his infantry from the center, along with a small number of cavalry. The remainder of the Persian cavalry was positioned on his right wing, along the shore.

As the battle opened, the strong Persian cavalry was able to push back the horsemen on the Macedonian left. On the right, Alexander led the Companion Cavalry in a typically aggressive charge against the Persian infantry, but the troops were well matched and the fighting was fierce. As Diodorus

This detail of the Alexander Mosaic shows Darius in his war chariot, leading his army at the Battle of Issus.

says, "the scales inclined now one way, now another, as the lines swayed alternately forward and backward. No javelin cast or sword thrust lacked its effect as the crowded ranks offered a ready target. Many fell with wounds received as they faced the enemy and their fury held to the last breath, so that life failed them sooner than courage."

Eventually, the Macedonians managed to break through the Persians' left-hand ranks, dividing Darius's troops. This move split apart the Macedonian phalanx, as well, briefly making it vulnerable to the Greek mercenaries fighting for Persia. But then, spotting Darius himself in his royal golden chariot, Alexander charged. Seeing the fierce Macedonian general rushing toward him, Darius fled the field—a move that left his troops in disorder and panic. As the Persians hastily attempted a retreat, their cavalry was hemmed in by the Macedonian phalanx. Meanwhile, thousands of their infantrymen (both Persians and mercenaries) were killed. Finally the bulk of Darius's troops escaped the field, but not before tens of thousands were killed, wounded, or taken prisoner.

TERRIBLE TACTICS

Many of the battles Alexander fought had extremely high death tolls, and his methods may seem terribly harsh, especially compared to modern standards. But in the ancient world, his tactics were not unusually aggressive. Ancient warfare was a vicious, bloody affair, and even the enslavement or imprisonment of large numbers of civilians was not uncommon.

SPOILS OF WAR

Alexander and his troops enjoyed the treasures left behind in the Persian army camp. Alexander even bathed in the Persian king's luxurious tub. However, he also showed compassion. Among the Persian captives were Darius's mother, his wife, and three of his children. When Alexander learned that the king's family believed that Darius had been killed, he went immediately to their tent. Assuring the grieving relatives that the Persian king was, in fact, alive, he also guaranteed them every honor befitting a royal family—except their freedom.

"NOT JUST A KING"

After the victory at Issus, Alexander continued to the south, deciding it was safest to secure Macedonian control over the entire eastern Mediterranean before moving farther east. Along the way, he received a letter from Darius, requesting the safe return of his family and offering rewards of money and land. Alexander refused. Because the Persians had first brought war to the Greeks, he said, "I am not the aggressor in this war, but acting in self-defence. Further-more, the gods support the better cause: I have already brought most of Asia under my control and defeated you in person in the field." He went on to say that, should Darius come to Alexander as a "suppliant"—that is, as a defeated party—his loved ones would be returned. Until then, Alexander's only additional advice was that "when you write to me remember that you are writing not just to a king, but to *your* king."

Skirting the sea, Alexander won the surrender of most of Phoenicia and Syria, at the eastern end of the Mediterranean. He continued to progress relatively quickly until January 332 B.C., when he reached Tyre. This Phoenician city, located in what would later become Lebanon was, like Halicarnassus, an important port. Located on a small, rocky island a short distance from the coast, it had great natural defenses, which were supplemented by high walls, dedicated troops, and a fleet of ships.

Taking this fortress would require creative tactics. Alexander promptly destroyed Old Tyre, which lay on the mainland. Using the stones of the demolished city, his workers began building a mole, or pier, from the shore to the walls of New Tyre. The work progressed slowly. A series of setbacks ranged from violent storms, attacks by Tyrean ships, and assaults from within the walls of Tyre. With grim determination, Alexander continued work on the mole.

As the siege wore on, stretching month after month, Alexander's stubbornness—while not out of character—might have come in part from the strange but promising dreams that came to him during the siege. At one point, he dreamed that the Greek mythic hero Hercules welcomed him to Tyre, offering a hand to the king and leading him inside the city walls. Another night Alexander dreamed of a satyr, a half-human, half-goat creature common in Greek myths. The beast "mocked at him from a distance and evaded his grasp when he tried to seize him, but . . . at last after much coaxing and pursuing, allowed himself to be caught," writes Plutarch. When Alexander questioned his philosophers and other advisors about the meaning of this dream, "the soothsayers gave a plausible interpretation . . . by dividing the word *sa-tyros* into two, to which they gave the meaning 'Tyre will be thine.'" Residents of Tyre also spoke of unusual dreams, including one—supposedly shared by several people—in which the god Apollo ominously abandoned the city.

Whatever the correct interpretation of such signs, Tyre's fate was finally decided in late summer of 332 B.C., after seven long months of siege. With the mole's construction complete at last, Macedonian battering rams and other siege engines were wheeled out near the city walls. As these weapons forced a break in the Tyrean defenses, a bloody struggle erupted in which six thousand to eight thousand Tyreans were—apparently with Alexander's approval—slaughtered within the city walls. The viciousness of this

Alexander and his army arrive in boats to attack the city of Tyre in this illustration from the fifteenth-century French book History of Alexander the Great.

massacre was extreme compared to the army's previous battles, given that the victims were trapped and posed no further threat. Historical sources offer two main explanations for this glimpse of Alexander's darker side. One is the length of the siege, which had taken the lives of a number of Alexander's men and left his other troops discouraged and weary. Secondly, some of those Macedonians who had been killed in attacks during the siege had been thrown into the sea from the top of Tyre's walls—thus depriving them of proper burial. This act of disrespect may have so enraged Alexander that he willingly allowed thousands of townspeople to be murdered, selling others—including women and children—into slavery.

Leaving the carnage of Tyre behind, Alexander pressed onward to Gaza, another holdout against the Macedonians. Yet another siege took place here, beginning in early fall—but the Macedonian soldiers, experts at siege tactics by this point, took the city in a span of fewer than three months.

TO THE LAND OF THE PHARAOHS

In late fall 332, having secured the whole eastern Mediterranean as planned, Alexander, age twenty-four, reached Egypt. The region's leaders promptly surrendered, and the Macedonians were welcomed as liberators. For although Persia had governed Egypt for close to two centuries, the empire's rule had never rested comfortably on this proud land. Egypt's ancient traditions often clashed with those of the Persians. In particular, the Persian kings Cambyses and Artaxerxes III, who led campaigns against

Egypt in the 500s B.C. and the early 300s B.C. respectively, had desecrated Egyptian temples and dishonored their deities. While Alexander, too, was a foreign ruler, he brought promises of a return to old Egyptian ways. In fact, one of his first acts in Egypt was to pay tribute to several Egyptian gods at the city of Memphis. The Egyptians viewed him as a savior instead of an enemy. In fact, they even hailed Alexander as a new pharaoh, and some historians believe they held a coronation ceremony shortly after Alexander's arrival.

Having taken possession of this stunning new prize, Alexander was eager to found a city in the region. It would not only serve as a reminder of his accomplishments, but

This detail from a larger fifteenth-century Italian painting shows Alexander's army and the construction of Alexandria, Egypt.

also occupy a strategic location as a port along the southern Mediterranean. After surveying several sites, he chose an appealing spot at the western edge of the Nile Delta, where Egypt's mighty river empties into the Mediterranean. He ordered construction of the city—which he named Alexandria—to begin at once.

PROPHECY AND PROPAGANDA

Alexander paid close attention to ancient traditions, legends, superstitions, and omens. He appears to have been quite devout himself, regularly making sacrifices to the gods. He was also well aware of the value of symbolism and religion for public relations.

For example, he made no secret of the legends that he was, through his father, a descendant of Hercules. He also strove to achieve the glory of legendary Greek heroes and drew parallels between himself and Achilles, the hero of the Trojan War.

In Egypt, Alexander's decision of where to found Alexandria was based, in part, on a dream, and he was temporarily troubled when flocks of birds began acting strangely near the construction site. While in Egypt, Alexander also took the opportunity to consult the famous oracle of Ammon (an Egyptian counterpart to Zeus), located at the oasis of Siwa. Siwa was deep in the desert west of Memphis, and the route across the sands was long and potentially dangerous. Sudden sandstorms had been known to swallow dozens of men at a time in this part of the desert. But no such disaster befell Alexander and his men. In fact, their journey was accompanied by mysteriously benevolent events, including birds that helped the group find its way through the unfamiliar landscape.

Once Alexander reached the shrine, "the high priest of Ammon welcomed him on the god's behalf as a father greeting his son"—hinting that Alexander's true father might be Ammon (Zeus) himself. Then, cutting to the chase, Alexander "proceeded to ask whether he was fated to rule over the entire world. The priest . . . answered that he was going to rule over all the earth."

According to Plutarch, Alexander also received one piece of information from Ammon that he kept secret, writing to his mother that he would share it with her when he returned to Macedonia. When that return might be, however, was something the king had failed to ask of the oracle. Newly reassured by his visit to Ammon, and with progress on Alexandria underway, Alexander left Egypt in the springtime of 331 B.C. Leading his army, he returned northward through Phoenicia and Syria, stopping to meet up with reinforcements from home. Then, in midsummer 331 B.C., he turned eastward—marching toward the center of Persia.

CHAPTER FOUR

"THIS COUNTRY PERSIA"

This country Persia . . . is a good country,
full of good horses, full of good men. . . .
[T]his country fears no other country.

—from an inscription of Darius the Great, king of Persia from 521 B.C. to 486 B.C.

The Persian Empire in the 300s B.C. was the largest that had yet existed in world history. Centered in modern Iran, the realm stretched eastward to the edges of India. To the west, it reached as far as the Mediterranean Sea, encompassing parts of modern-day Turkey north of the Mediterranean and controlling Egypt and Libya to the south. It was these westernmost borders that threatened Greek power, leading to the Persian Wars of the fifth century B.C.

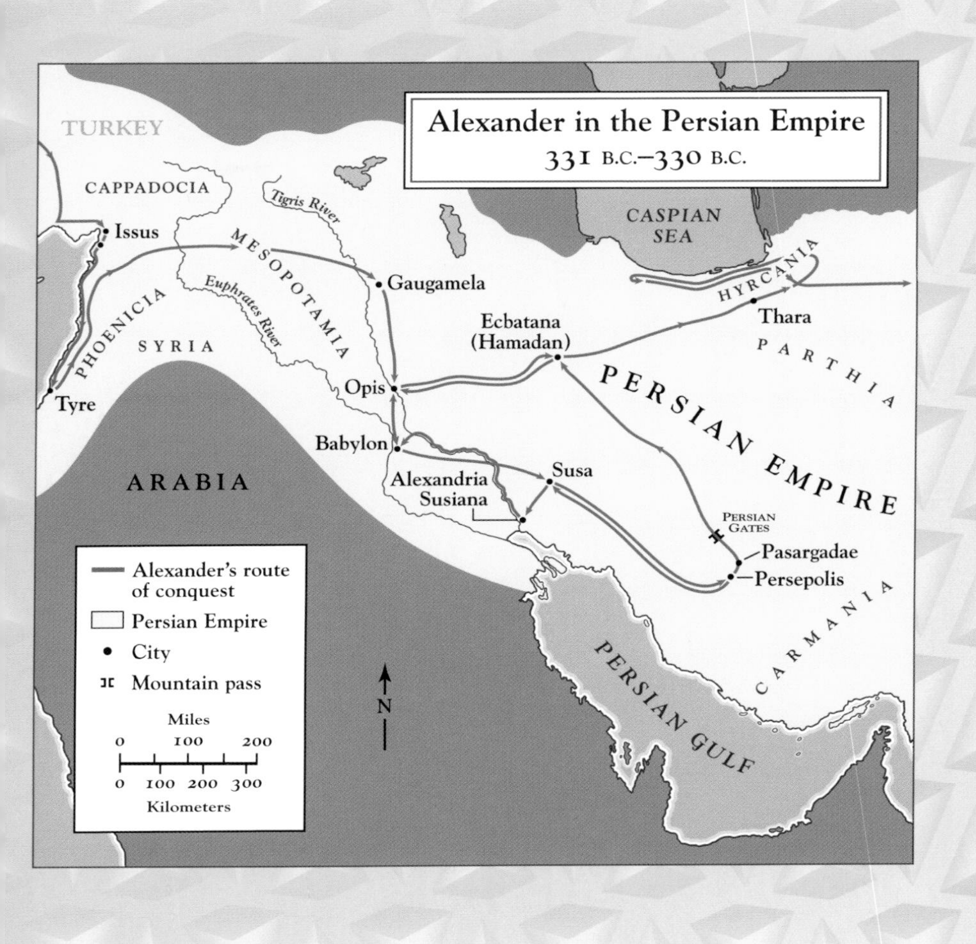

This vast empire held a wide array of climates, terrains, and peoples. In addition to a variety of ethnic groups who were native to the heart of Persia, peoples conquered by the Persian Empire over the years numbered more than seventy in all, and included the Medes, Parthians, Bactrians, Babylonians, Assyrians, and Egyptians. Not surprisingly, these subjects spoke many languages. The most common were Aramaic, Median, and Old Persian (a relative of modern-day Farsi, the language of Iran).

ROYAL ROAD

The Persian Empire's important centers were connected by the Royal Road, running more than 1,500 miles (2,400 kilometers) from east to west. A network of smaller roads kept distant regions in touch.

In Alexander's time, all of these peoples and territories were ruled by the Achaemenid dynasty. The first prominent Achaemenid ruler was Cyrus the Great, who took power over the realm from the Medes (of northern Iran) in 559 B.C. Later, Darius I (Darius the Great) expanded the empire significantly. By the time of his rule, the realm was so large that it had three separate capitals—Persepolis, Susa, and Pasargadae. And as the empire continued to grow and flourish, Persia itself became a tempting prize for outside invaders.

THE GREAT KINGDOM

At the top of the Persian government was the king, often called the Great King of Persia. These rulers generally claimed hereditary power, taking the throne through succession when another dynasty member died. The Great King was honored—among other ways—by *proskynesis*, time-honored Persian customs of showing respect to superiors. Bowing was one part of the tradition, in which people of inferior rank bowed to those in higher positions. Persian subjects bowed all the way to the floor in front of the Great King. Another aspect of proskynesis was a kiss the king bestowed on honored members of the court.

Next below the supreme level of Great King came regional governors called satraps. Each satrap—whose title was a Median word translated as "protector of the realm or land"—governed over a satrapy, or province, and reported to the king. A satrap had many duties, ranging from tax collection to judging criminal trials and maintaining peace and safety in the satrapy. He did not carry out all of these jobs alone, of course. An extended staff of lower-ranking officials, administrative workers, and troops from the empire's army assisted him in his day-to-day tasks.

Satraps had a great deal of power within their own realms, and the position was at risk for abuse. Given this danger, plus the great distance between some satrapies and the capitals, Persian rulers did not always feel they could trust their satraps. To guarantee their reliability, the kings employed agents called the "eyes and ears of the king."

This marble frieze from the fourth century B.C. was found in Turkey. It shows two men approaching the throne of a Persian satrap. An attendant shades the ruler with an umbrella, as bodyguards stand by.

These employees were government spies of a sort, hired by the king to check up on his satraps and to ensure their loyalty and freedom from corruption. Even so, with a hold on their regions' purse strings, troops at their command, and a tantalizing taste of power, some satraps did launch rebellions against the central government. Very few came close to actually taking the throne. But their efforts were enough to send ripples of fear all the way to the king.

Despite such internal scuffles, the Persian Empire of the Achaemenids was by and large a prosperous and well organized kingdom. And although some Greeks thought of Persia as an uncultured, primitive land, this view was far from accurate. In fact, by the time Alexander arrived in the late fourth century B.C., the Persians already had a long and healthy tradition of justice. In the 500s B.C., the king Cyrus the Great had introduced a statement pledging that he would allow his subjects to continue following their own faiths and other traditional practices. Some historians view this document as the world's first official charter of human rights.

In keeping with these ideas, Persian rulers also explored a relatively new style of conquest. Persia had not acquired its

Now that I put the crown of kingdom of Iran, Babylon, and the nations of the four directions on the head . . . I announce that I will respect the traditions, customs and religions of the nations of my empire and never let any of my governors and subordinates look down on or insult them.

—from the charter of Cyrus the Great, 500s B.C.

> There is no nation which so readily adopts foreign customs as the Persians. Thus, they have taken the dress of the Medes, considering it superior to their own; and in war they wear the Egyptian breastplate. As soon as they hear of any luxury, they instantly make it their own.
>
> *—from Herodotus's "On the Customs of the Persians," 431–425 B.C.*

vast territory peacefully. One after another Persian kings led military campaigns to conquer greater areas. But some Persian leaders sought to take possession of lands with minimum strife—not by exercising greater force, but by practicing a measure of tolerance. Instead of obliterating the customs and beliefs of conquered peoples, the Persians absorbed many new traits from their subjects. While some Persian kings were harsher than others, the tactic proved quite successful overall. The result was a rich variety of peoples leading diverse lifestyles under a single ruler.

OLD AND NEW BELIEFS

Just as the Persian Empire was home to many different peoples, it was also a center of different religious beliefs. Ancient faiths had survived throughout the realm, due largely to the terms of Cyrus's charter. Most people worshipped a large pantheon (group) of deities, many of whom had control over a natural element, such as the seas, wind, or fire.

However, by the time of the Achaemenids, many Persians are believed to have followed a relatively new faith known as Zoroastrianism, founded by the Persian prophet Zoroaster. Zoroastrianism was different from the old faiths in many ways. For starters, earlier Persians, ancient Greeks, and most other cultures at the time were polytheistic—believing in multiple deities. Zoroaster, on the other hand, preached the existence of one supreme, omnipotent god called Ahura Mazda. Other immortal and holy beings also populated the Zoroastrian belief system, but these creatures were seen as powerful angel-like spirits rather than full-fledged gods.

Religious officials called magi oversaw the rites and rituals of Zoroastrian worship. Although many details of the role they played in ancient times have been lost, among their duties may have been the interpretation of dreams and omens. Other practices included the sacrifice of animals—as well as offering grains, fruit, wine, and other items, to Ahura Mazda. Fire was the central symbolic element of Zoroastrian rites, representing the truth and light of Ahura Mazda.

Magi also played a role in government. In ancient Persia, kings were believed to rule by divine right. This idea—that the empire's kings, while not gods themselves, were chosen by god—made church and state inseparable. And by surrounding himself with magi, who were the most

A great god is Ahura Mazda, who created this earth, who created yonder sky, who created man, who created happiness for man, who made Xerxes king, one king of many, one lord of many.

—from the Daiva inscription by Persian king Xerxes I (reigned 485–465 B.C.)

familiar symbols of the faith, a king strengthened his claim to divine authority.

A modern form of Zoroastrianism is still practiced, although it has a relatively small following. Most worshippers live in India and Iran. Zoroastrianism's sacred text, the Avesta, includes prayers, descriptions of rites and customs, and hymns.

HOME AND AWAY

With territory stretching from Egypt to Turkey to India, there was really no such thing as a "typical" Persian lifestyle. But in the heart of the empire, in modern-day Iran, certain common customs were shared.

Most Persian families lived in two-story homes built from handmade mud bricks, often painted white or in pastel colors and topped with a wooden roof covered in reeds. A high wall enclosed many homes, often sheltering a private garden that might include rose bushes, citrus trees, and fountains or ponds.

Achaemenid kings were said to throw extravagant banquets, with tables groaning under every kind of delicacy. For average Persians, mealtime was a more modest affair, including hearty starches such as barley, wheat, lentils, and beans. Rice was eaten in the empire's easternmost lands, while chickpeas were popular in the north. Supplementing these staples were foods including cheese, yogurt, fresh vegetables, meat such as lamb or beef, and fish. Sweet, fresh dates were a standard accompaniment to almost any meal, while a wide variety of other fruits, from pomegranates to pears, might serve as a light dessert. Diners often drank wine, which was sometimes made from dates instead of grapes.

Family was very important to the ancient Persians. Men were permitted to be polygamous (have multiple wives), and community values encouraged this custom. Having many children—particularly sons—was an important mark of status.

It is difficult to say what Persian wives and mothers thought of polygamy. But Persian women did have greater freedom than many other women in ancient times. For example, it was common for Persian women to hold jobs, and some advanced to high-ranking and well-paying positions—even earning enough to buy property of their own. And in parts of the empire, women held positions of minor political authority. Most Persian girls did not attend school, however. Instead, they usually stayed home to learn the duties of keeping a household. Boys generally did attend school, beginning around the age of five, but they also usually learned the family business from their fathers.

Many Persian subjects were employed as merchants and traders. A booming exchange of goods was carried on throughout the empire's territories and even beyond. Caravans trundled along the network of royal roads, carrying goods such as rugs and spices.

TRICKS OF THE TRADE

In part to smooth trade transactions, Persian kings improved banking systems throughout the empire. They also introduced standard weights and measurements. One was the cubit, a unit of length equal to approximately 18 inches (46 centimeters).

Many other Persians worked at farming. But the lowliest jobs in the empire were done by slaves. Some of these captives had been taken prisoner in war, while others were arrested as rebels or debtors. They labored at construction projects in particular, such as building the roads that kept the Persian Empire running.

AN EYE FOR BEAUTY

During the centuries of Achaemenid rule, the arts experienced a period of growth and refinement in Persia. The products of this flowering reflected Persia's diverse and wide-ranging culture at the time.

Architecture was an important artistic pursuit in Persia. Perhaps the grandest achievement of Achaemenid architects was Persepolis, the imperial capital of Darius I and later

Archaeologists began excavations of the city of Persepolis in 1931. The ruins speak to the grandeur of the city in its time.

kings. This great city contained magnificent temples, imposing government buildings, and a massive palace complex.

Inscriptions were carved into stone walls, tablets, and even mountainous rock faces throughout the empire, usually proclaiming imperial statements. Most were in cuneiform, a writing system of wedge-shaped characters that could be

This silver tablet with cuneiform writing from the fifth century B.C. was found in Iran. It defines Darius I's empire in three languages.

used for several different languages. Along with parts of the Avesta, these inscriptions comprise some of ancient Persia's only written works to have survived the centuries.

Another art form in ancient Persia was dancing. Some traditional dances had religious or other meaning, but many were simply for entertainment. Female and male court dancers performed for the royal family, and no Persian celebration was complete without dance.

AN UNCERTAIN FUTURE

In the mid-300s B.C., Achaemenid Persia was a vast, varied, and powerful empire. Its diverse peoples lived together under a relatively stable government. Good organization and a strong economy had brought the realm great territory and wealth.

However, the larger Persia grew, the greater risk there was for cracks in its foundations. Some of the empire's conquered lands chafed under Persian rule, and a lack of reliable troops led to the hiring of huge numbers of mercenary soldiers. Instability had grown in 358 B.C., when the king Artaxerxes III seized the throne by killing his rivals—including most of his family. This bloody beginning was just a taste of what was to follow during the twenty years of Artaxerxes' reign, which would be among the most violent of the Achaemenid period.

In 336 B.C., King Darius III took power through a tangled web of plots, poisoning, and intrigue. The Persian Empire had been a formidable foe for centuries, but its hold on power seemed to be growing shakier. And its greatest challenger yet was on his way.

CHAPTER FIVE

INTO THE HEART OF PERSIA

It is war that will determine the boundaries of our respective empires and each shall have what the fortunes of tomorrow assign to us.

—*Alexander in a message to Darius, according to Rufus, A.D. 31–41*

Following the Battle of Issus, Darius had hurried back to central Persia, where he began rebuilding his shattered army in preparation for another battle against Alexander. Now, in summer 331 B.C., Darius left Babylon (in modern Iraq) at the head of an enormous force.

Meanwhile, Alexander had sent Parmenio and a small force ahead to build a bridge across the Euphrates River. The king followed with the bulk of his army, marching his men through Mesopotamia (in modern Syria and Iraq) and establishing control over the region. Rejoining Parmenio, the troops crossed first the Euphrates and then the Tigris River. These great waterways, which fed the plains of western Persia, formed a fertile valley, where human communities flourished as early as 7000 B.C. This area came to be known as the "cradle of civilization."

As the Macedonian army continued eastward, its scouts learned that Darius was not far away. Alexander paused, allowing his troops to rest for a few days before meeting the Persians in what was sure to be a great struggle. Then, in the autumn of 331, the armies of Alexander and Darius clashed again, at the Battle of Gaugamela. Alexander was twenty-five years old.

Alexander and his army cross the Tigris and Euphrates rivers in this fifteenth-century French manuscript illustration from the History of Alexander the Great *by Quintus Curtius Rufus.*

A VAST ENEMY

Gaugamela lay on the plains of what later became northern Iraq. Darius wisely stopped here on his march from Babylon, choosing this wide, open field to make his stand. He knew that the terrain would favor his massive army—believed by historians to be at least as big as the one at Issus, and probably somewhat larger—and put Alexander's forty-five thousand to fifty thousand Macedonian troops at a disadvantage.

One night shortly before the battle, as the armies each were encamped a few miles apart, Plutarch reports that Parmenio "looked out . . . and saw the entire plain agleam with the watch-fires of the barbarians, while from their camp there arose the confused and indistinguishable murmur of myriads of voices, like the distant roar of a vast ocean." Daunted by the vastness of the enemy, Parmenio reportedly suggested to Alexander that perhaps he should attack by night—to which Alexander replied, "I will not steal my victory." The king "was determined that if Darius were defeated . . . he was not to be allowed to blame darkness and night for his failure."

So the Macedonians readied themselves for battle on a morning in early fall. The Persian troops were already waiting on the field. Darius's army this time relied much more heavily on cavalry than it had at Issus, with a relatively small number of infantrymen. At the front of the Persian ranks were more than one hundred scythed chariots—regular war chariots equipped with long blades that extended from each wheel.

Alexander drew up his men in the usual arrangement, with the phalanx placed front and center. Confronting the long line of the Persian cavalry, however, Alexander adjusted his setup somewhat. He curved his own line of troops slightly, stationing small groups at each end in order to prevent the Persians from wrapping around the Macedonian troops and attacking from behind. As further insurance, Alexander placed an extra battalion of infantry behind the main line.

As the battle opened, Alexander directed his right wing to move farther to the right, against the Persians' left wing. As Alexander's men continued to move outward from the center, they forced Darius to stretch his line to meet their attacks. Eventually a gap opened in the Persians' left wing, and Alexander, leading a wedge-shaped unit of Companion Cavalry, charged swiftly against the weakened spot. The distinctive shape of the charge was extremely effective. Using a small number of men in the front of the wedge exploited the opening in the line efficiently. They widened the gap to let the soldiers behind them push through in greater numbers.

As they crashed through the Persian line, Alexander and his men engaged in vigorous close-quarters combat. Then, spying Darius in the chaos of the field, Alexander charged against him as he had at Issus. But before he could engage the king in hand-to-hand combat, Darius fled the field, frustrating Alexander, who had hoped to kill or capture the Persian king once and for all. Alexander began to pursue the king and the troops who followed him. But he was stopped when he received a message from Parmenio, who—in dire straits with the left wing—had sent a call for help. The Macedonian cavalry along the left flank had been unable to stop the much larger Persian force, which had quickly gained the upper hand and encircled the left Macedonian flank. But rather than attacking from the rear, some of the Persians galloped on behind the line toward the Macedonian camp, where they may have hoped to rescue Darius's family. The Persians pillaged and burned the camp, leaving many dead. Parmenio was left struggling against additional squadrons of Darius's cavalry, while the back of Alexander's troops remained vulnerable.

Heeding the distress call, Alexander wheeled around and rushed to his cavalry's aid. As he cut back through the Persian line and approached his own, he trapped a group of Persian soldiers. "The ensuing struggle," Arrian writes, "was the fiercest of the whole action; one after another the Persian squadrons wheeled in file to the charge; breast to breast they hurled themselves on the enemy. Conventional cavalry tactics . . . were forgotten; it was every man for himself, struggling

French painter Jaques Courtois chose Alexander defeating Darius at the Battle of Gaugamela as the subject of this seventeenth-century painting.

to break through as if in that alone lay his hope of life. Desperately and without quarter, blows were given and received, each man fighting for mere survival without any further thought of victory or defeat."

Then, as news spread through the Persian lines that their king had fled, formations disintegrated completely, and the rest of the army took flight. When the dust had settled, an estimated one thousand Macedonians lay dead. The Persians had lost fifty thousand or more.

THE RICHES OF BABYLON

Gaugamela represented a stunning defeat for Darius—one that seemed to represent a final change of fortune for the Persian army, and for the empire itself. Alexander, it appeared, was now the king of Asia—which, in the ancient Greek view, made him virtually the king of the entire world. As he headed deeper into Asia, towns fell before him without a fight, and satraps offered up the riches of their kingdoms.

At Babylon, for example, Mazaeus—a Persian leader who had commanded and fought gallantly at Gaugamela—surrendered the ancient city willingly. In fact, according to Arrian, Alexander "was met by the people of the place who with their priests and magistrates came flocking out to bring him various gifts and to offer to put the city, with the citadel and all its treasures, into his hands." Meanwhile, Rufus reports, the city treasurer, Bagophanes, "had carpeted the whole road with flowers and garlands and set up . . . silver altars heaped not just with frankincense but with all manner of perfumes."

RUNNING THE REALM

Alexander, advancing rapidly through Asia, generally spent little time in conquered areas to set up new governments and other systems himself. However, he knew that a poorly run empire was destined to fall. As he continued on in search of the next victory, he trusted the management of his newly won territories to his officers. Assisted by troops, these administrators also helped deal with unrest, such as an uprising that occurred in Sparta as Alexander advanced toward Gaugamela.

Alexander also made a practice of rewarding leaders who surrendered their territory. He often placed them in prominent posts, sometimes even making them governors of their former realms. In addition, he generally provided them with a garrison of troops and a few administrators. To keep his own army at full strength, Alexander periodically sent for reinforcements.

Although these descriptions may have been embellished somewhat, Alexander did occupy Babylon without a struggle. Diodorus puts it more simply: "The people received him gladly."

In return for such hospitality, Alexander paid his respects to the city's history and culture, arranging for the rebuilding of the grand temple of Bel-Marduk. This monument had served as a fortress in wartime as well as an honor

This strategy had several benefits. First, it encouraged leaders to surrender, knowing that they would probably be rewarded for the decision. Secondly, it allowed Alexander to suggest that he supported the local people and believed that they should govern themselves. But by leaving his own soldiers and officers behind, Alexander also ensured the security of his territory.

Another effect of this system was that Greek and Macedonian soldiers settled throughout Asia, introducing local people to the Greek language and customs. Alexander also introduced Greek currency in all of his conquered lands, as well as establishing a trade network throughout the realm. All of these changes resulted in the rapid spread of Greek culture throughout Alexander's Asian conquests.

to the supreme Babylonian god, Marduk. It had been destroyed by the Zoroastrian leader Xerxes. Probably to show that he was more benevolent, Alexander made sacrifices to Marduk in Babylon.

Babylon turned out to be so pleasant that Alexander and his troops rested there for more than a month. Then, in early winter, he moved the army to Susa, which lay eastward in modern-day Iran. The city was one of the centers of the

THE TREASURES OF SUSA

Persian architecture drew on resources from throughout the realm—and even from beyond, through the network of Persian trade routes. As Darius recounts in an inscription on the walls of his Susa palace: "This palace which I built at Susa, from afar its ornamentation was brought. . . . The gold was brought from Sardis and from Bactria. . . . The silver and ebony were brought from Egypt. . . . The ivory which was wrought here, was brought from Ethiopia and from Sind and from Arachosia. . . . The stone-cutters who wrought the stone, those were Ionians and Sardians. The goldsmiths who wrought the gold, those were Medes and Egyptians."

empire—and, as such, held one of Persia's richest treasuries. But when the Macedonian army arrived, the city's commander handed over the town, and Alexander "entered . . . without opposition and took over the fabulous palace of the kings." Within the walls of Susa, Alexander found, as expected, a fortune, including thousands of talents (ancient monetary units) worth of gold and silver.

Ahead, however, lay a still greater prize: Persepolis, another capital of the Persian kings. Rumor had it that Darius had taken refuge there. Alexander could follow one of two routes to Persepolis. The easier path followed the Royal Road, which ran southward and avoided the steepest part of the mountains that rose along the way. But this route would take a long time—long enough for the Persians to evacuate Persepolis, taking with them most of the city's treasures. The shorter way, through the mountains, required traveling through a narrow and well-defended pass known as the Persian Gates.

Alexander decided on a twofold tactic. He sent Parmenio along the Royal Road with most of the army as well as the supplies. At the same time, Alexander himself led a smaller, fast moving force to the Persian Gates. When he reached the pass in midwinter 330 B.C., it was guarded by about forty thousand men. Despite the odds against them, the Macedonians launched an attack. They were trapped at the bottom of the narrow gorge and nearly defenseless, while the Persians, stationed above, rained down arrows, slingshot stones, and boulders. The Macedonians were driven back—though not without taking several prisoners.

Retreating and making camp, Alexander called these prisoners before him and questioned them, hoping to learn something of his enemy's weaknesses. One provided him with a crucial piece of information: a little-known path through the mountains led to the other side of the pass, where the Persian camp lay. As the Persians would never expect the Macedonians to know of or follow this route, Alexander's men could catch the enemy by surprise.

Alexander left his general Craterus in charge of most of the troops at the camp. Then, under cover of darkness, led by the prisoner, Alexander and a light force moved off along the secret path. It was a difficult journey, as, "apart from the impossible crags and precipitous rocks that time and again made them lose their footing, their progress was further impeded by snow-drifts, into which they fell as if into pits. . . . Night and the unfamiliar landscape also multiplied their fears." But by dawn, the group had neared the enemy camp. With Craterus back at the Macedonian camp and waiting for Alexander's signal, Alexander gave the order for the assault to begin. Arrian writes, "As he fell upon the trench, the trumpets sounded, and Craterus, accordingly, immediately moved to the assault . . . on the other side. The enemy were properly caught."

Having taken the pass, Alexander moved swiftly on toward Persepolis. According to Justin, Alexander, "Marching forward in quest of the enemy," had always "kept the soldiers from ravaging Asia, telling them that 'they ought to spare their own property, and not destroy what they came to possess.'" For the most part, indeed, Alexander did not pillage or burn the lands through which his army passed. One exception to this restraint, however, was Persepolis. When the Macedonians entered the city early in 330 B.C., Alexander gave his men permission to pillage the city's homes, and his soldiers killed many residents. In addition, Alexander himself is said to have led his troops in one final act of destruction, setting the great palace of the capital aflame.

Some historical authors claim that Alexander intended all along to destroy Persepolis as revenge for the burning of Athens during the Persian Wars. Others say that he got the idea during a rowdy victory party. According to this story, women who traveled with the army joined this particular party and an Athenian woman named Thais, who was the mistress of Alexander's general Ptolemy, convinced Alexander to set fire to the city. Her urging went against the better judgment of Parmenio and other advisors, who considered the move rash, needlessly destructive, and certainly bad for the army's reputation. Whatever the king's reasons may have been, he left smoldering ruins behind him in Persepolis. As Rufus writes, "such was the end of the palace that had ruled all the East."

PURSUING THE FOE

With Persepolis and the surrounding regions in his control, Alexander moved on in late spring 330 B.C. He turned to the northwest, toward the city of Ecbatana (modern Hamadan, Iran), where Darius had earlier fled. Although experience had convinced the Persian king that his chances against Alexander were slim, he was determined to make one final stand. First, however, he hoped to reinforce his diminished army with additional troops from satrapies in the East. As Alexander advanced, Darius headed for the region of Bactria, in modern-day Afghanistan. Alexander arrived in Ecbatana in early summer, and learning of Darius's new direction, he followed.

A treasonous plot drastically changed Darius's plans. Bessus, the powerful satrap of Bactria, had convinced a number of his fellow leaders to support him in a plan to arrest the king. He intended to hand over Darius to Alexander, thus earning the Macedonian conqueror's favor—and, he hoped, keeping Alexander from conquering Bactria and the other eastern satrapies.

But Alexander wanted no part of such a deal. Killing Darius in heroic battle was one thing. Accepting him from a traitor—and at the cost of the valuable eastern empire, no less—was something else altogether. So when he learned a few weeks later that Bessus had, indeed, taken Darius prisoner, Alexander drove his troops eastward at as swift a pace as the army could stand. His goal was to catch and fight Bessus, thus putting an end to any chance of an agreement. But the journey was grueling, passing through the dry lands of northern Iran at the height of summer. At one point on the march, Plutarch recounts, Alexander "met some Macedonians, who were carrying water from a river in skins on the backs of their mules, and when they saw Alexander almost fainting with thirst in the midday heat, they quickly filled a helmet and brought it to him." The king, however—a master of theatrical gesture—refused the gift. "Alexander took the helmet in his hands. But then he looked up and saw the rest of his troops craning their heads and casting longing glances at the water, and he handed it back without drinking a drop. He thanked the men who had brought it, but said to them, 'If I am the only one to drink, the rest will lose heart.' However no sooner had his companions witnessed this act of self-control and magnanimity than they cried out and shouted for him to lead them on boldly. They spurred on their horses and declared that they could not feel tired or thirsty or even like mortal men, so long as they had such a king."

But even after covering more than 200 miles (322 km) in less than two weeks, Alexander had not caught up to Bessus. Each town the Macedonians reached, it seemed, the Persians had just left. Finally, with a small, lightly armed force of his toughest men, Alexander made a final push, traveling 50 miles (80 km) in one night. With the Macedonians now bearing down on him at an alarming speed, Bessus panicked and repeatedly stabbed his captive near the Parthian town of Thara (east of present-day Tehran, Iran). Leaving Darius half-alive along the road, where he probably expected Alexander to find the body, Bessus and the Persian troops continued on toward Bactria.

When Alexander and his men came upon the dead king riddled with javelin wounds and lying abandoned in a wagon, Alexander was reportedly saddened by the man's fate. Covering him, Plutarch says, with his own cloak, he arranged for Darius to have a royal funeral.

This Persian miniature from the fifteenth century shows a Persian-style Alexander kneeling beside the body of Darius.

Darius's death—while it was the very thing Alexander had hoped to achieve in battle—now presented a problem. Most of Alexander's troops saw it as the end of their mission to Asia. Eager to return to their homes, they began packing up camp. But Alexander had no intention of turning back. In his view, the riches of Bactria and beyond still lay before him. And he could hardly allow Bessus—who had now declared himself king under the name Artaxerxes V—to go free. To claim the title of Persia's king for himself, Alexander had to get rid of this pretender to the throne.

Determined to march onward, Alexander rallied the Macedonian troops with a rousing speech—and some extra pay. Newly inspired, they prepared to set off after Bessus.

CHANGING WAYS

Alexander and his troops continued northward into Hyrcania. On the march, they reached the shore of the Caspian Sea, catching "sight of a bay of the open sea which appeared to be as large as the Black Sea and was sweeter than the Mediterranean." In this pleasant land, Alexander accepted the surrender of several of Darius's former satraps and commanders.

The army next marched through the region of Parthia, still in pursuit of Bessus. It was around this time, as they moved farther east, that Alexander adopted several Persian customs. He began to wear elements of Persian dress, including long white robes and colored sashes, and he crowned himself with Persia's traditional royal headdress, called a diadem. Eventually he also tried to introduce proskynesis, the Persian custom of showing honor to superiors—and especially the Great King—through ceremonial bowing and kisses.

STIRRING SPEECH

"Men! If you consider the scale of our achievements, your longing for peace and your weariness of brilliant campaigns are not at all surprising. Let me pass over the Illyrians, the Triballians, Boeotia, Thrace, Sparta, the Achaeans, the Peloponnese—all of them subdued. . . . Just look! Beginning the war at the Hellespont, we have delivered Ionia and Aeolis from subjection to the insolent barbarian, and we have in our power Caria, Lydia, Cappadocia, Phrygia, Paphlagonia, Pamphylia, Pisidia, Cilicia, Syria, Phoenicia, Armenia, Persia, the Medes, and Parthiene. I have subjugated more provinces than others have captured cities, and in my calculations I may have forgotten some because of the very numbers involved!

Consequently, men, if I believed that our grip on the lands we have so swiftly conquered were sufficiently firm, I would certainly break loose from here . . . back to my home . . . and the rest of our countrymen, so that there especially I could enjoy the reputation and glory I have won with you, in that place where the richest of our rewards for victory are waiting for us—joyful children, wives and parents, peace and quiet, the carefree possession of what our valour has won. But our empire is new and, if we are prepared to admit the truth, insecure; the barbarians still hold their necks stiff beneath the yoke. . . . So we must either let go what we have taken or seize what we do not yet hold."

—Speech given by Alexander in 330 B.C.

These Persian guards are dressed in robes like the ones that Alexander began wearing. This fifth-century B.C. *relief was found in Persepolis.*

Another major change came as Alexander began to integrate Persian men into the royal court and the army. He added Persian women to the mix, as well. Darius's 365 concubines joined the already large group of people that traveled with the army.

Most of the Macedonians and Greeks found such changes offensive. They were embarrassed at seeing their own king engaging in such "barbaric" practices. To these proud warriors, the idea of shedding their own traditions in favor of the customs and costume of the very people they had conquered seemed ridiculous and undignified. In addition, proskynesis was especially troublesome, as in Greece and Macedonia such physical humbling and reverence would be performed only in religious worship. Alexander's troops saw proskynesis as treating the king as a god. Therefore, Alexander's acceptance and encouragement of such reverence seemed intolerably prideful.

The question of why Alexander chose to introduce these changes has been puzzled over for centuries. Some historians believe that victory had made Alexander vain, while others say that he was spoiled by Persian decadence. These views could, at least to some extent, have been correct. The young king—just twenty-six years old—may easily have been drawn to the more "exotic" luxuries of this unfamiliar land that he had claimed as his own. His arrogance may have made honors such as proskynesis seem very attractive.

But Alexander might also have believed that these actions were politically necessary. After all, if he were indeed going to declare himself to be the legitimate successor to Darius's throne, shouldn't he embrace some of the customs of the Great King of Asia? And if he commanded the proper respect among his new subjects through traditional rites such as proskynesis, wouldn't his control over those subjects be more secure? In addition, Alexander may have felt that showing an appreciation for Persian culture would do far more good for his rule than dismissing or diminishing it. In places such as Egypt, he had seen for himself the harm that the Persian kings had done by dishonoring the closely held beliefs of different cultures.

Some of the ancient authors believed that such practical aims were at least part of Alexander's thinking. As Plutarch says, the king "tried to reconcile Asiatic and Macedonian customs: he believed that if the two traditions could be blended and assimilated in this way his authority would be more securely established when he was far away, since it would rest on goodwill rather than on force."

CHAPTER SIX

TO THE ENDS OF THE EARTH

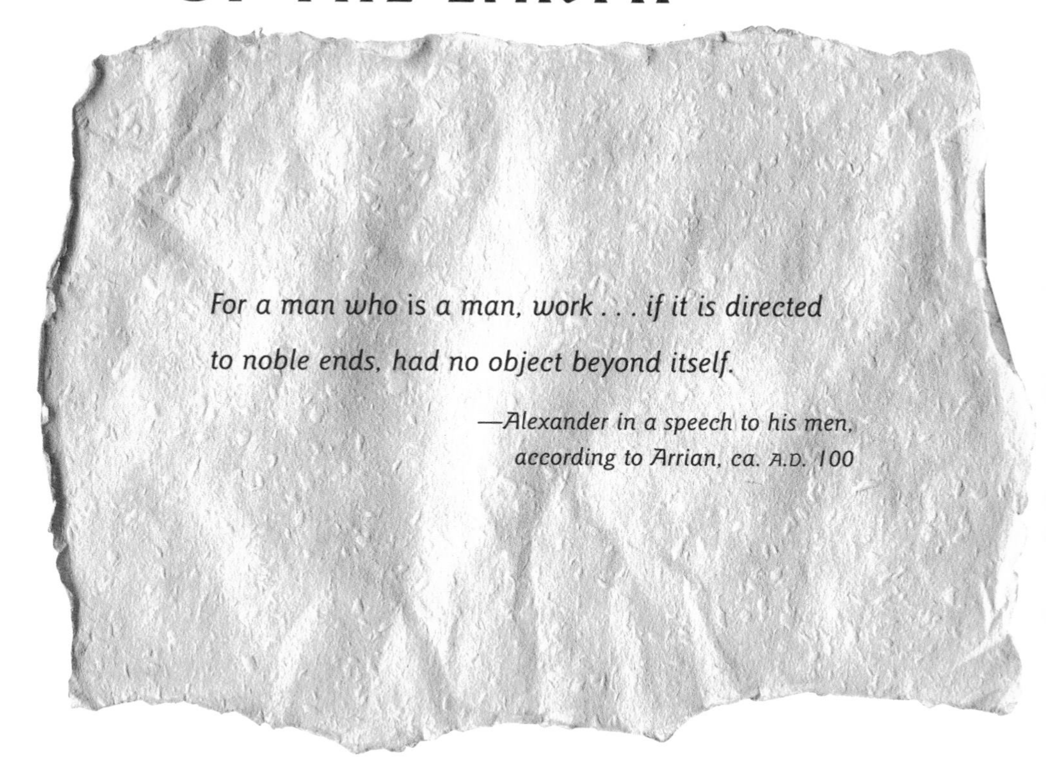

Pushing ever farther into Asia, Alexander passed through Aria and into Drangiana, part of southern Afghanistan in modern times. The army took possession of these areas with little trouble, as opposition there was minimal and easily subdued.

The army next turned northward into the province of Arachosia. Following the Helmand River Valley through the region's mountains, they next reached the satrapy of

Gandara (near modern Kabul, Afghanistan). The journey had been a hard one, through rugged land and bitter winter weather, and the troops stopped briefly in Gandara to recover. But as usual, the break was soon over. At this point, little of Darius's former empire remained unconquered. But Bactria and Sogdiana were still free—and fiercely determined to remain so. Alexander was equally determined to make them his.

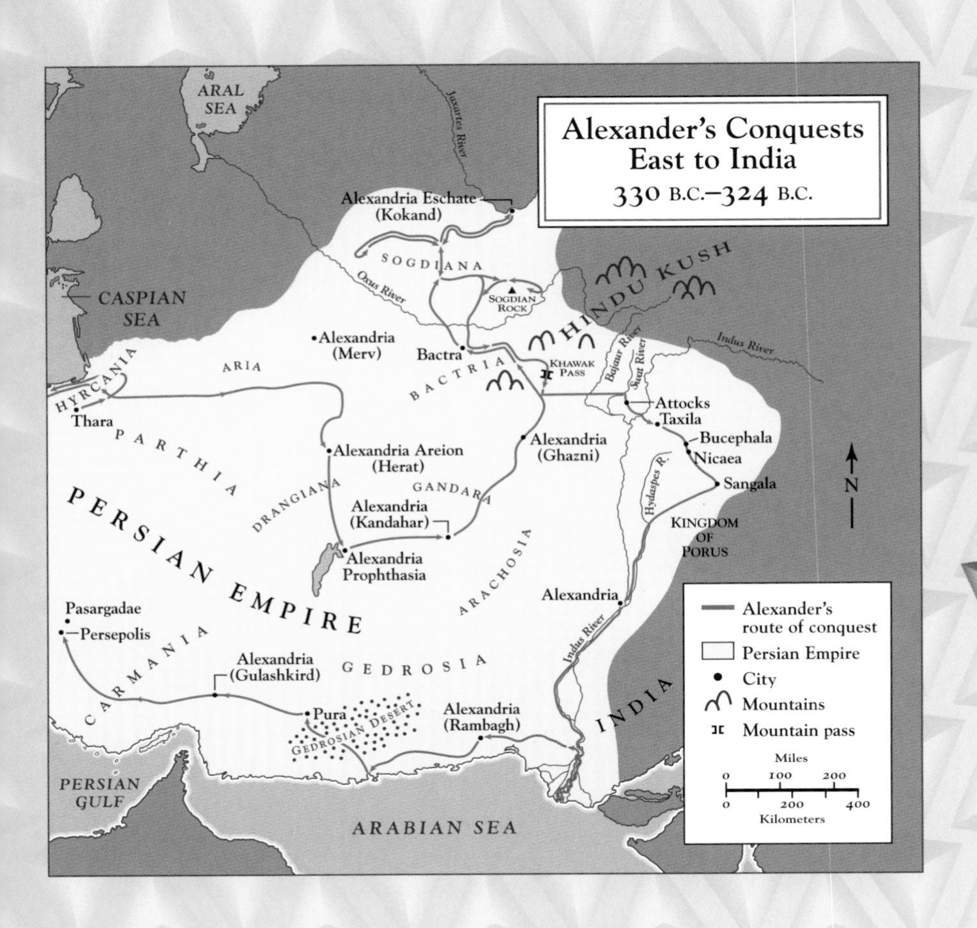

ACROSS THE HINDU KUSH

To reach these regions—and Bessus, who still ruled over Bactria—Alexander would have to cross the barrier of the Hindu Kush. This mountain range, stretching across northern Afghanistan and into Pakistan, is craggy and snow-covered, with peaks reaching heights of more than 25,000 feet (7,620 m). The high, narrow passes that offered the only way through the range were treacherous and choked with snow in all but the summer months.

Seemingly undaunted by the challenge, Alexander began the crossing in early spring, 329 B.C. According to Rufus, the march, which led the army through the mountains via the Khawak Pass, took just seventeen days. But it was a grueling trip. Bitter wind whipped around the soldiers,

The snow-blanketed Hindu Kush as it looks in modern times

and snow drifts blocked their way. Many of the army's horses died of exposure and exhaustion. Supplies were desperately short. Bessus had ordered his troops "to lay waste the country round the foothills of the [mountains], in the hope that if all crops and everything edible between Alexander and himself were destroyed, Alexander would be halted by sheer lack of supplies. The hope, however, was vain; Alexander, in spite of everything, continued to advance."

Upon emerging in Bactria on the other side of the Hindu Kush, Alexander found Bessus still beyond his reach. As Alexander had drawn closer, Bessus and his men had decided to cross the Oxus River, which bounded Bactria to the north. The Oxus was not far away. So Alexander stopped again to allow his exhausted army a few days of rest, then he led them onward to the river.

Between the mountains and the Oxus lay a dry, rugged landscape. Temperatures soared as the troops marched northward, and food shortages were still a problem. But Alexander pushed his troops on. By the time he reached the Oxus in early summer, many of his men had died from dehydration, and some of the Greek soldiers had simply quit and headed for home. In a last attempt to keep the Macedonians at bay, Bessus had burned all available ships and boats. Having already destroyed most trees in the area, he left virtually nothing for his enemy to use in crossing the mighty river, which ran fast and deep. But still, nothing would stop Alexander. Drawing on the few supplies they had, his soldiers crafted makeshift rafts out of tents filled with hay and sewn tightly closed. Floating across the great waterway on these unconventional vessels, the army landed in Sogdiana.

By this time, the forces Bessus had assembled had seen enough. Terrified by Alexander's seemingly unstoppable advance, they seized Bessus and surrendered him to Alexander. Sending the captive to Ecbatana for justice, Alexander—acting in the manner of a Persian ruler—ordered that Bessus should suffer the traditional Persian penalty for regicide (killing a king). The unlucky prisoner had his nose and ears cut off before being publicly executed.

Even with Bessus out of the picture, unrest and rebelliousness against Alexander's rule still seethed in Bactria and the surrounding areas. Aiming to subdue the region once and for all, Alexander pressed on northeastward into Sogdiana, heading for the very edge of Darius's empire: the Jaxartes River. Called the Syr Darya in modern times, the river marked the northernmost point of Alexander's campaigns. He founded a city along the Jaxartes, in what is now Tajikistan, and named it Alexandria-Eschate: Alexandria the Farthest.

Turning southward again, Alexander and his troops moved through Sogdiana and Bactria. Encountering resistance and revolts all along the way, the Macedonian campaign in this region stretched from the autumn of 329 B.C. into spring 327 B.C. For every local leader who offered willing submission, another seemed to rise up against Alexander. One prominent leader, Spitamenes, had originally become an ally only to turn against the Macedonians later, organizing troublesome revolts. In these independent northern regions, residents employed guerrilla tactics, using small forces to strike at the Macedonian troops in surprise hit-and-run attacks. This type of warfare was relatively unfamiliar to Alexander's army, posing yet another challenge.

Alexander himself was wounded in several of the conflicts of this long campaign. Once he was shot in the lower leg, and the arrow broke his fibula bone. Another time he was struck in the face with a stone—an injury that temporarily left him with impaired sight and speech. He also contracted gastroenteritis, an intestinal disease, while near the Jaxartes River. For everyone, even the king, the years of warfare were taking their toll.

FIERCE CRIMES AND FLYING MEN

One evening during a break from the campaigning in Sogdiana and Bactria, in the autumn of 328 B.C., Alexander and his comrades were relaxing and enjoying a banquet. Most of the guests, who included some of Alexander's Asian recruits, were speaking—and drinking—freely. But the mood was less friendly than it first appeared.

Some authors say that the trouble began when Alexander started boasting about his successes as well as belittling the achievements and character of his father, Philip. Others recount that flatterers at the party were comparing Alexander to the legendary hero Hercules, while Alexander did nothing to silence the extravagant praise.

Whatever the exact subject matter was, it was deeply distasteful to Cleitus. As co-commander of the Companions, he was a prominent and well-regarded officer, and a very old friend of Alexander and his family. Cleitus had also saved Alexander from almost certain death in the first war against the Persians. But Cleitus had grown disgusted with what he saw as Alexander's intolerable vanity, as well as his adoption of Persian ways. Now he could not hold his tongue. Such talk "grossly exaggerated the marvellous nature of Alexander's achievements, none of which were mere personal triumphs of his own," Cleitus spat out, according to Arrian. "On the contrary, most of them were the work of the Macedonians as a whole."

Stung by the remark, Alexander responded with insults of his own. The argument escalated rapidly, each man hurling harsh words at the other. Suddenly, Alexander reached for a weapon. Several of his officers moved to restrain him, while others pulled Cleitus from the room. But within a few terrible moments, Alexander had run Cleitus through with a spear.

This terrible act stunned Alexander's men—and the king himself, it seemed. In the shocked and silent moments after the deed, he seemed to come to his senses. Horrified by what he had done, he retired to his own quarters. Plutarch writes, "There he spent the rest of the night and the whole of the following day sobbing in an agony of remorse. At last he lay exhausted by his grief." After several days during which the king shut himself away and refused food, his concerned officers convinced him to eat and begged him to forgive himself. One philosopher in the royal court even told him that the acts of a great king were never wrong, and that he was above the laws that guided common men. This advice—which may have been intended mainly to win Alexander's favor—seemed to help, and Alexander finally roused himself and returned to work.

Ongoing unrest in Bactria and Sogdiana was partially solved when Spitamenes was killed by nomads after he fled to the desert late in 328. But major conflicts still lay ahead.

THE ALCOHOL QUESTION

Some ancient authors claim that Alexander was a heavy drinker, especially in his later years. Rufus recounts that "Alexander had some great natural gifts: a noble disposition surpassing that of all other monarchs; resolution in the face of danger; speed in undertaking and completing projects; integrity in dealing with those who surrendered and mercy towards prisoners; restraint even in those pleasures which are generally acceptable and widely indulged. But all these were marred by his inexcusable fondness for drink." Some accounts blame both the burning of Persepolis and the murder of Cleitus on drunkenness. Plutarch, on the other hand, directly denies such claims, stating that Alexander was "more moderate in his drinking than was generally supposed. The impression that he was a heavy drinker arose because when he had nothing else to do, he liked to linger over each cup, but in fact he was usually talking rather than drinking." Whether Alexander was or was not an alcoholic will probably never be known.

Warriors at several area fortresses continued to resist. Around the beginning of 327 B.C., Alexander's troops headed to one of these fortresses, known as Sogdian Rock. It was a cold and miserable winter march, during which many soldiers died. The surviving troops arrived at their goal in early spring to find an imposing fortress town with steep rock cliffs on all sides.

One story of this operation tells that Alexander offered the inhabitants mercy if they surrendered. Oxyartes, the commander of the Rock, replied with taunts, telling Alexander that, unless he had winged soldiers, he would never take the fortress. Never one to back away from such a challenge, Alexander asked three hundred of his men most skilled in climbing for volunteers to scale the Rock. All three hundred answered his call, and they set off under cover of darkness. Tied together with ropes and using iron tools to dig into the rock walls, they scaled the steep face. About thirty men fell to their deaths in the snow below. But the rest, Arrian says, "reached the top as dawn was breaking, and the summit of the Rock was theirs. Then, in accordance with Alexander's orders, they signaled their success to the troops below by waving bits of linen, and Alexander sent a crier to shout the news to the enemy's advanced posts that they might now surrender without further delay, as the men with wings had been found and were already in possession of the summit. And, as the crier gave them this information, Alexander pointed to his men, where they stood on top of the Rock." The enemy, stricken with fear at seeing what they had thought was impossible, promptly surrendered the city to Alexander.

Among the town's residents was Roxana, the daughter of Oxyartes. This young woman, renowned for her beauty, apparently caught Alexander's eye. When he informed Oxyartes that he wished to marry Roxana, her father was more than happy to agree to such a match. Roxana and Alexander were married in the summer of 327 B.C.

This marriage was politically advantageous to Alexander and may have been nothing more than a way to

Alexander the Great marries Roxana, daughter of Oxyartes, in this dramatic eighteenth-century painting by Italian artist Mariano Rossi. Alexander is dressed in a traditional Greek tunic, while Roxana is clothed as an eighteenth-century beauty.

win favor among his new subjects. In addition, the connection with Oxyartes—who was a powerful regional leader—helped Alexander subdue the rest of the area. At the same time, many of the ancient sources claim that the king was genuinely in love with his new bride. The truth may well have been somewhere in the middle. As Rufus puts it, Alexander "fell in love with a young girl, of humble pedigree in comparison with royalty, and did so with such abandon as to make a statement that intermarriage of Persians and Macedonians would serve to consolidate his empire." Whatever the case, twenty-nine-year-old Alexander was

newly married, thousands of miles from home—and on the verge of a still more ambitious project.

THE LURE OF THE SEA

With the Persian Empire under his control, Alexander now set his sights on a more exotic prize: India. According to ancient ideas of India's geography, the Great Ocean that encircled the world lay not far beyond the Indus River (located near India's northwestern border). Imagining India, therefore, as a narrow peninsula between the Indus and the ocean, Alexander probably thought it would be no great challenge to conquer it. After all, he and his men had already claimed the greatest empire in the world.

Before leaving for India, Alexander took precautions to protect the edges of his realm. Creating a number of towns along these borders (and naming them all Alexandria), he left substantial forces to guard the frontiers. Then, after bulking up his army with reinforcements—many of them Asian—Alexander headed southward once more, making a return crossing over the Hindu Kush.

The late spring crossing of the mountains was still challenging, but a far less lethal journey than the first. Arriving back in Bactria for the summer, Alexander sent messages ahead to a number of Indian leaders to negotiate their surrender. Some—many of whom ruled small, independent communities with few troops compared to the massive Macedonian army—did submit without a fight. Some even arrived with gifts to please their new ruler, and Alexander asked several of these men to stay and serve as guides for the army.

The next step was to conquer those who had not surrendered. In autumn 327 B.C., Alexander launched a two-pronged approach to the task. He sent Hephaestion with most of the cavalry and infantry, along with most of the supply train, ahead to the Indus. Hephaestion had orders to subdue the region between Bactria and the river and to make arrangements for the army to cross the Indus.

Meanwhile, Alexander himself took a smaller force on a more northern route, through the Bajaur and Swat river valleys. In this area, he would encounter some of the fiercest resistance of his entire career. The mountain tribes around the rivers had no intention of surrendering, and their warriors were skilled and brave. Alexander himself received several injuries during this campaign, including an arrow wound to the shoulder. Perhaps realizing what a worthy foe he faced and hoping to prevent opposition in the first place, Alexander used harsh tactics in taking the towns of the area. In one of the first conflicts of the campaign, he instructed Craterus "to strike terror right at the start into a people which had, as yet, no experience of Macedonian arms" and "to show no mercy." But even with this harsh opening, resistance remained intense. The operations that followed—lasting through the winter of 327 B.C. and into 326 B.C.—were fierce and bloody.

Several incidents during this period were rumored to be signs of Alexander's divinity—that he was not just descended from the gods, but a god himself. One was the capture of Nysa, a town associated with the god Dionysus. Alexander also laid siege to a fortress north of Attock, which, the rumors said, even the divine hero Hercules had failed to defeat. The Macedonians, however, succeeded. So, Arrian wrote, "Alexander was left in possession of the Rock which had baffled Heracles [Hercules] himself." Whether or not Alexander himself believed this interpretation is unknown, but it seems that he was willing to let such stories circulate.

As he pushed on toward the Indus, Alexander accepted the surrender of Ambhi, the raja (king) of the Taxila region. Ambhi came bearing lavish gifts. But Alexander—reluctant to be outdone in any way—returned the gifts and added some of his own. In addition to publicly demonstrating Alexander's generosity, this move was intended to ensure that Ambhi remained an ally.

Alexander knew of two primary foes who remained: the rajas Porus and Abisares. Receiving advance reports that Porus was already gathering an army at the Hydaspes River, east of the Indus, Alexander moved to meet him there.

Alexander and his troops reached the Indus in spring 326 B.C., rejoining the rest of the army. Continuing eastward, they reached the banks of the Hydaspes. Waiting for them were Porus and an Indian army of approximately forty thousand men.

A HEROIC FOE

Porus—a brilliant military officer as well as a powerful regional leader—was perhaps the most able enemy Alexander had yet fought. In addition, in this battle the Macedonian army faced a weapon that they had little experience against: war elephants. Although Alexander had gained some elephants of his own from defeated foes on his way to the Hydaspes, his troops had little idea of how to combat them. The elephants frightened the horses of Alexander's cavalry with their unfamiliar appearance and smell—and did a good job of intimidating Alexander's men, too, as it turned out. Rufus reports, "The Macedonians were alarmed not only by the appearance of their foes but also by the size of the river. . . . The bank supplied an even more terrifying scene, covered as it was with horses and men and, standing among them, those immense bodies with their huge bulk . . . these [elephants] deafened the ears with their horrendous trumpeting. The combination of the river and the enemy suddenly struck terror into hearts which were generally given to confidence and had often proved themselves in battle." Porus himself also cut an imposing figure. He "rode an elephant which towered above the other beasts. His armour,

A fifteenth-century edition of Quintus Curtius Rufus's History of Alexander the Great *includes this illustration of Alexander facing Indian war elephants.*

with its gold and silver inlay, lent distinction to an unusually large physique. His physical strength was matched by his courage."

Similar to Alexander's first great battle, at the Granicus, his troops now faced the challenge of crossing a large river. But this waterway—at least near the armies' camps—was even wider and swifter, and simply charging across would be impossible. Rafts would not work, either, as the horses would be too terrified by the elephants to cooperate.

While his scouts looked for alternative crossing points, Alexander tried to keep the enemy guessing. He ordered additional food to be brought in, making it seem that he would be encamped for a while. At the same time, he had his men carry out training drills and other preparations, implying that an attack might be coming soon.

Finally, having found a suitable island for a crossing, Alexander decided on his plan. Leaving Craterus in charge of a large group of troops at camp, he continued to keep the Indian forces off guard by having the soldiers raise a commotion periodically, but not make any real moves to attack. At first, Porus roused his troops and readied for battle. But as time went on and nothing happened, Porus let his men rest.

Meanwhile, a detachment of about fifteen thousand cavalry and infantry, led by Alexander, moved to the crossing point, about 15 miles (24 km) from camp. Other units stationed themselves between camp and the crossing point.

At dawn the next morning, Alexander led his men across the Hydaspes. As he arrived on the opposite bank, a chain of Indian scouts alerted Porus to the situation. Porus sent approximately two thousand troops and several dozen chariots, led by his own son, hurrying down the bank to counter Alexander. But the group was too small.

Alexander's larger force obliterated the Indian detachment, and Porus's son was among the dead. In response, Porus left part of his force—along with a number of elephants—to guard against a crossing by Craterus and sent the rest to confront Alexander. With this move, the real battle began.

Porus advanced on Alexander with his elephants in front and infantry behind, flanked by cavalry and chariots. Alexander, still unable to lead his cavalry directly against the elephants, instead sent most of his cavalry against the left wing of Porus's cavalry. The powerful Macedonian cavalry attack drew Porus's right-wing cavalry to the left wing to help, but it wasn't enough. The Indian horsemen were pushed back against the elephants, where they had no good escape. Meanwhile, Alexander's javeliners and archers had been attacking the elephants and their handlers. Now that the Indian cavalry was in trouble, Alexander's phalanx advanced on the elephants. Arrian describes a terrifying scene, as "the monster elephants plunged this way and that among the lines of infantry, dealing destruction in the solid mass of the Macedonian phalanx." But as some of the phalanx pushed through the elephants to engage the Indian infantry, the elephants, frightened, injured, and crowded from all sides, began doing harm to their own army. "As they blundered about, wheeling and shoving . . . they trampled to death as many of their friends as of their enemies." Soon the Macedonians had Porus's force mostly surrounded, and thousands were killed. Meanwhile, Craterus's men crossed the river and prevented any escape in the direction of camp.

A victorious Alexander is shown with the wounded Porus in this detail from an oil painting made by Charles Le Brun in the seventeenth century.

With victory in hand but fighting still in progress, Alexander moved to make sure that Porus was not killed. Alexander respected the king's courage, for, "unlike Darius, he did not lead the scramble to save his own skin, but . . . fought bravely on." Alexander sent a messenger to Porus, offering mercy, and the Indian king—wounded and exhausted—accepted.

A CHANGE OF PLANS

After the Battle of the Hydaspes, Craterus and a small group stayed behind to oversee the construction of Bucephalia and another new city. Meanwhile, Alexander and most of the army headed eastward. He planned to take control of the

FRIEND AND COMRADE

After the Battle of the Hydaspes, Alexander's horse Bucephalus died. Wounded and weary, the steed had, Arrian writes, "shared with Alexander many a danger and many a weary march." The king held a large funeral for the noble animal. Plutarch reports, "Alexander was plunged into grief . . . and felt that he had lost nothing less than a friend and comrade. He founded a city on the banks of the Hydaspes and called it Bucephalia."

entire region up to the shores of the Great Ocean, which he still believed to be nearby.

The army did easily seize most of the area, accepting surrender from several dozen towns. Around this same time, messengers arrived from the raja Abisares, announcing his surrender and an offer of friendship and cooperation. But other enemies proved harder to defeat. Further resistance from local peoples slowed the army's progress. The town of Sangala proved especially hard to defeat, but finally ended with the city's capture—and a toll of more than fifteen thousand Indian deaths. The people of neighboring towns, rather than accept terms for surrendering to the Macedonians, fled—and Alexander followed. As Arrian writes, "so long as a single hostile element remained, there could, [Alexander] felt, be no end to the war."

Not everyone felt the same way. As the army continued through India, morale among the average phalanx and infantry soldiers had sunk farther and farther. India was hot, utterly unfamiliar, and filled with wildlife unlike any the men had seen before. After years of battle and no return home, the army's uniforms, sandals, and even weapons were in poor shape—not to mention being constantly wet. The Macedonians had been unlucky enough to travel through the region during the rainy monsoon season, and they had endured steady rainfall ever since the Hydaspes. Weary, underequipped, and homesick, they were unable to understand why their commander led them ever onward, especially when the original goal of Persia had long since been attained. In fact, Arrian writes, "The sight of their King undertaking an endless succession of dangerous and exhausting enterprises was beginning to depress them. Their enthusiasm was ebbing." To make matters worse, there was no sign that the Great Ocean they were seeking was drawing any closer. After eight years and 11,000 miles (17,700 km) on the road, the troops reached their breaking point in the summer of 326 B.C. While camped east of the Hydaspes River, their growing dissatisfaction was reported to Alexander.

The king attempted to change their minds with a speech similar to the one he had given after the death of Darius. He reminded them of the many victories they had won already and of the glory that would accompany further conquests. He also urged them not to risk losing the territories they possessed by not finishing the job.

But this time, inspiring words were not enough. The crowd of soldiers was silent, until many—so weary and full of longing to see their homes and families again—began to weep. Finally one of Alexander's officers, Coenus, spoke up on behalf of the men. He was diplomatic but frank, stressing the troops' loyalty to Alexander but also their exhaustion. Rufus writes that Coenus pleaded, "Look at our bodies—debilitated, pierced with all those wounds, decaying with all their scars! Our weapons are already blunt; our armour is wearing out." As Coenus finished, the army showed their approval of his words, bursting into applause. But Alexander, stung by the reality that his men were no longer willing to follow him, still would not give in. "'I shall have others,' he cried, 'who will need no compulsion to follow their King. If you wish to go home, you are at liberty to do so—and you may tell your people there that you deserted your King in the midst of his enemies.'"

Alexander then retired to his tent in a huff. Staying there for three days, he refused any and all visitors. But it was too late for such melodrama. The troops would not be swayed. Finally, Alexander sent word that he would, indeed, turn homeward. At this announcement, Arrian records, "One can imagine the shouts of joy which rose. . . . Most of [the soldiers] wept. They came to Alexander's tent and called down every blessing upon him for allowing them to prevail—the only defeat he had ever suffered."

HOMEWARD BOUND

During the Indian campaigns, Alexander had ordered a fleet of ships to be built, both for river battles and, probably, in preparation for reaching the Great Ocean. Some boats had been captured, as well. Now Alexander prepared to sail this fleet down the Hydaspes River, continuing down the Indus after the rivers met, and on southward to the Indus delta. If he could not reach the ocean to the east, he would at least travel south to see it. At the Great Ocean (actually the Arabian Sea), the army would turn westward, toward home. By late fall 326, they set off down the river. Two columns of soldiers marched along the riverbanks, while the fleet sailed ahead between them.

Although they were finally heading home, the army was not done fighting. A number of battles broke out with local peoples living in the regions around the river on the way to the sea. At this point, the battles had become still more violent between Indians fiercely determined to protect their homes and Macedonians desperate to return to theirs. Thousands of Indians were killed in assaults on towns and fortresses, and Alexander, Diodorus says, "spread the terror of his name throughout the whole region."

In one of these battles, Alexander was shot with an arrow that struck his chest near his lung. The surgery to remove the arrowhead was so dangerous that many of the troops were sure their king would never survive. In fact, as the army continued to move southward, with Alexander recovering on one of the ships, a rumor spread that he had already died. The unrest this news caused drew Alexander from his sickbed. Arrian describes a dramatic scene as the king's ship came to shore. "Alexander raised a hand in greeting to the men, and immediately there was a shout of joy. . . . As he was being moved from the ship, a party of his Guards brought him a stretcher; but he refused it and called for his horse. He mounted, and at the sight of him, once more astride his horse, there was a storm of applause so loud that the river-banks and neighbouring glens re-echoed with the noise. Near his tent he dismounted, and the men saw him walk; they crowded round him, touching his hands, his knees, his clothes."

Continuing along the Hydaspes and the Indus, Alexander divided the army in early summer 325 B.C. He sent Craterus and a large division marching west to Arachosia, while the rest continued southward to the ocean. Alexander may have had several reasons for making this decision. One was an intention to use supplies most efficiently by sending troops through different parts of the empire. In addition, Craterus was charged with the task of subduing unrest that had risen in some of the satrapies. A third reason, however, had less to do with military strategy. The ancient sources suggest that some competition had arisen between Craterus and Hephaestion. Craterus was unquestionably the better officer, but Alexander seemed to want to promote Hephaestion to higher ranks. As Plutarch put it, "In general, he showed great affection to [Hephaestion], and great respect to [Craterus], for he believed—and always said—that Hephaestion loved Alexander, but Craterus loved the king." In any case, by separating the troops, Alexander was able to give Craterus's old position to Hephaestion.

When the rest of the army neared the ocean, Alexander sent the fleet, under the command of his admiral Nearchus, sailing westward along the coast. Alexander and most of the troops, meanwhile, moved westward on land, not far from shore. They planned to dig wells to supply fresh water for both themselves and the fleet. But Alexander's route, through Carmania and Gedrosia (southern Pakistan in modern times), included dangerous desert regions. It soon became clear that both water and food were scarce. And when the army reached the Talar-i-Bund mountains, forcing them to march farther inland, they lost touch with the fleet. There may have been a planned meeting that never took place. But, this development left them with desperately limited supplies. As the troops marched on through the scorching desert, famine set in. The starving men took to slaughtering their pack animals, but even this measure was too little. Disease tore through the ranks, as well, and thousands died of hunger, sickness, and thirst.

This nightmarish journey finally ended when the army reached the Gedrosian city of Pura, but as many as sixty thousand lives had been lost. Grief-stricken, angry, and possibly eager to find someone to share the blame for this devastating march, Alexander turned on the regional satraps for not sending aid. Whether they were at fault is unknown, but several were arrested and executed. Meanwhile, news of unrest in other parts of the empire brought further worry. One of the most distressing stories concerned an official named Harpalus, who had been left in charge of the army's treasury—and seemed to have been dipping into the funds for himself. After many intrigues, he was killed after fleeing to Crete.

In the winter of late 325 B.C. and early 324 B.C., the troops led by Craterus, Nearchus, and Alexander all met in Carmania. After a short rest, the entire army set out once again. Nearchus would continue as commander of the fleet (now sailing through the Persian Gulf), while Hephaestion led troops along the coast and Alexander marched farther inland, toward the Persian city of Pasargadae. The three branches would meet again in Susa.

At Pasargadae, Alexander visited the tomb of the great Persian king Cyrus—only to find it vandalized and emptied of its riches. Furious, Alexander blamed the satrap of Pasargadae's region for not preventing the crime. The unfortunate man was arrested, tried, and ultimately hanged.

The harshness of this punishment may have stemmed from Alexander's desire to stress that he would not tolerate any disrespect of a Persian king—himself included. But even beyond this incident, Alexander seemed to have grown increasingly sensitive and fearful about threats and disloyalty. This fear then led to increasingly rash acts, more vicious

The tomb of Cyrus the Great that Alexander visited in 324 B.C. still stands in modern-day Iran, near the ruins of the ancient Persian capital of Pasargadae.

tactics in battle, and outbursts of temper. Arrian says simply that he was "quicker to take offence."

Some historians believe that Alexander's ego—and, possibly, a growing belief on his part that he was a god—had taken control over his reason. According to these scholars, Alexander was now driven by blind ambition and a belief that he was both invincible and above justice. Another theory is that the pressures of controlling his vast empire had grown too great, leading to fearful reactions and overly strict measures. And the genuine unrest within the army—strengthened by Alexander's unpredictable behavior—fed his own paranoia at the same time.

CELEBRATIONS AND SORE SPOTS

When the troops reunited in Susa in spring 324 B.C., they enjoyed a much needed rest. They also attended a great celebration. While at Susa, Alexander arranged marriages between about eighty of the Companions and Persian women of prestigious birth. Alexander himself married Barsine, a daughter of Darius, and also Parysatis, daughter of Ochus. These matches, combined with his marriage to Roxana, tied Alexander into three of the most powerful families in Persia. For Hephaestion, he chose Barsine's sister as a bride, "as [Alexander] wanted to be uncle to Hephaestion's children."

The mass celebration was partly strategic, designed to intertwine Macedonian and Greek bloodlines with noble Persian families. But it was not entirely unwelcome. In fact, as many as ten thousand of Alexander's men already had Persian wives. As an added benefit, every couple received generous gifts, and the festive five-day occasion included a fabulous banquet.

The marriages, however, did little to dispel the trouble still brewing over the issue of Persian influence on Alexander and his court and army. Persian replacements had long been a source of tension. Particularly unnerving to Alexander's original men was a huge group of about thirty thousand young Persian recruits whom Alexander had chosen to receive Macedonian-style military training. The king also ordered that these men learn Greek language and culture. The older Macedonian troops wondered if these youths would become the core of their king's army.

Knowing that such worries plagued his men, Alexander took further measures to improve morale, such as paying off the debts of all his soldiers. Nevertheless, in late summer 324 B.C., a crisis erupted when at Opis (a city on the Tigris River, north of Babylon). Alexander offered to send the wounded and oldest Macedonians home immediately, while the rest would continue to carry out small campaigns on the way back to Greece. But rather than welcoming the chance, Alexander's most trusted old soldiers felt they were unwanted. Worst of all, they felt that they were being dismissed in favor of newer, younger Persian troops. So, far from inspiring thanks, Alexander's announcement instead brought open complaints and even jeering from his troops. Enraged at such disrespect, the king jumped down from his platform into the crowd and had several of the most vocal soldiers arrested. He then gave a fiery lecture to the men, speaking yet again of their successes and fortunes under his leadership, and of his own constant place right alongside them. As

he had at the Hydaspes River, he shut himself away in his quarters and refused to see anyone. According to Arrian, "on the third day he sent for the Persian officers who were in the highest favour and divided among them the command of the various units of the army. Only those whom he designated his kinsmen were now permitted to give him the customary kiss [as part of proskynesis]."

These actions by Alexander were probably meant to strike real fear and hurt into the hearts of the Macedonians, already insecure about their king's regard for them. It worked. The old officers came to their king's quarters, pleading for his forgiveness. According to Arrian, they "swore they would not stir from the spot day or night unless Alexander took pity on them. Alexander, the moment he heard of this change of heart, hastened out to meet them, and he was so touched by . . . their bitter lamentations that the tears came into his eyes." One Companion spoke up, saying, "'My lord . . . what hurts us is that you have made Persians your kinsmen. . . . But no Macedonian has yet had a taste of this honour.' 'Every man of you,' Alexander replied, 'I regard as my kinsman, and from now on that is what I shall call you.'" As his men came forward to receive the ceremonial kiss, harmony once again seemed restored.

GRIEF

The army moved to Ecbatana for the summer of 324 B.C. In autumn of that year, Hephaestion fell ill with a high fever and died barely a week later. Alexander had lost the friend of whom he had once said, "This man is Alexander too."

Arriving at Hephaestion's bedside, Alexander was mad with grief. He stayed by the body, weeping, for many hours and refused food or comfort for two days. When at last he could be led away, he cut his hair short, as Achilles had done after the death of his dearest friend, Patroclus. He had the body sent on to Babylon for burial, and Diodorus writes that he "showed such zeal about the funeral that it not only surpassed all those previously celebrated on earth but also left no possibility for anything greater in later ages."

After the funeral and other honors for Hephaestion, Alexander moved on in the winter of 324 B.C. He launched a campaign against the Cossaeans, a people in the mountains southwest of Ecbatana. This assault was extremely harsh, and many ancient historians speculated that Alexander was driven to extra aggressiveness by his ongoing grief for Hephaestion. Whatever the cause, however, the Cossaeans suffered for it. Leaving all these tragedies behind, Alexander pushed onward to Babylon.

FAREWELL TO A KING

On the road to Babylon, the Macedonians met representatives of lands as far away as Italy. These ambassadors offered Alexander gifts—probably hoping he would go home and not bother them. Another group, however, came bearing only a warning. The Chaldeans, a highly regarded group of Babylonian scholars and seers, arrived to inform Alexander that they foresaw his death if he came into Babylon. When the king heard the prophecy, Diodorus writes, "he was alarmed and more and more disturbed, the more he reflected."

Alexander even set up his own camp outside the city walls when they arrived at Babylon in early spring 323 B.C. But when his philosophers—surprised by his uncharacteristic nervousness—convinced him not to worry, he joined the rest of his men in the city and put his fears aside.

Alexander spent the spring receiving additional ambassadors. He also may have been planning another great expedition—possibly as soon as summer. He seems to have been especially drawn to the promise of the Arabian Peninsula. Then, in spring, the king was enjoying festivities commemorating, in part, the death of the hero Hercules. Very suddenly, Alexander fell ill. Some sources, such as Diodorus, state that he drank a large cup of wine and suddenly "shrieked aloud as if smitten by a violent blow." Others say that the king simply

Far behind me lie
those golden-rivered lands, Lydia and Phrygia,
where my journeying began. Overland I went,
across the steppes of Persia where the sun strikes hotly
down, through Bactrian fastness and grim waste
of Media. Thence to rich Arabia I came;
and so, along all Asia's swarming littoral
of towered cities where Greeks and foreign nations,
mingling, live my progress made.

—from The Bacchae, *by Euripides, 404 B.C. (spoken by Dionysus, a Greek god sometimes associated with Alexander)*

felt a bit sick at the end of the night. In either case, when Alexander awoke the next day, he was gripped by fever. For several days, he did little but bathe—probably in an attempt to keep cool—and rest in his room. But still the king's condition worsened. His strength was declining, his fever was rising, and he grew less and less able to speak. The doctors were called in but seemed unable to help. Finally, both Alexander and his men sensed that the end was near.

At this point, Arrian reports, the troops were so worried for their leader that "nothing could keep them from a sight of him, and the motive in almost every heart was grief and a sort of helpless bewilderment at the thought of losing their king." Accordingly, a second door was made for Alexander's room, so that his men could pass through for what they knew would probably be a last look at their king. "Lying speechless as the men filed by," Arrian says, Alexander "yet struggled to raise his head, and in his eyes there was a look of recognition for each individual as he passed."

Finally, Alexander gathered his highest officers. When they asked who his successor should be, he replied, according to some accounts, that his kingdom should go to "the strongest," while others translate his words as "the best." And on June 10 or 11, 323 B.C., Alexander the Great died. He was thirty-three years old. "At first," writes Rufus, "the sounds of lamentation [and] weeping . . . echoed throughout the royal quarters. Then a sad hush fell, enveloping all in a still silence like that of desert wastes."

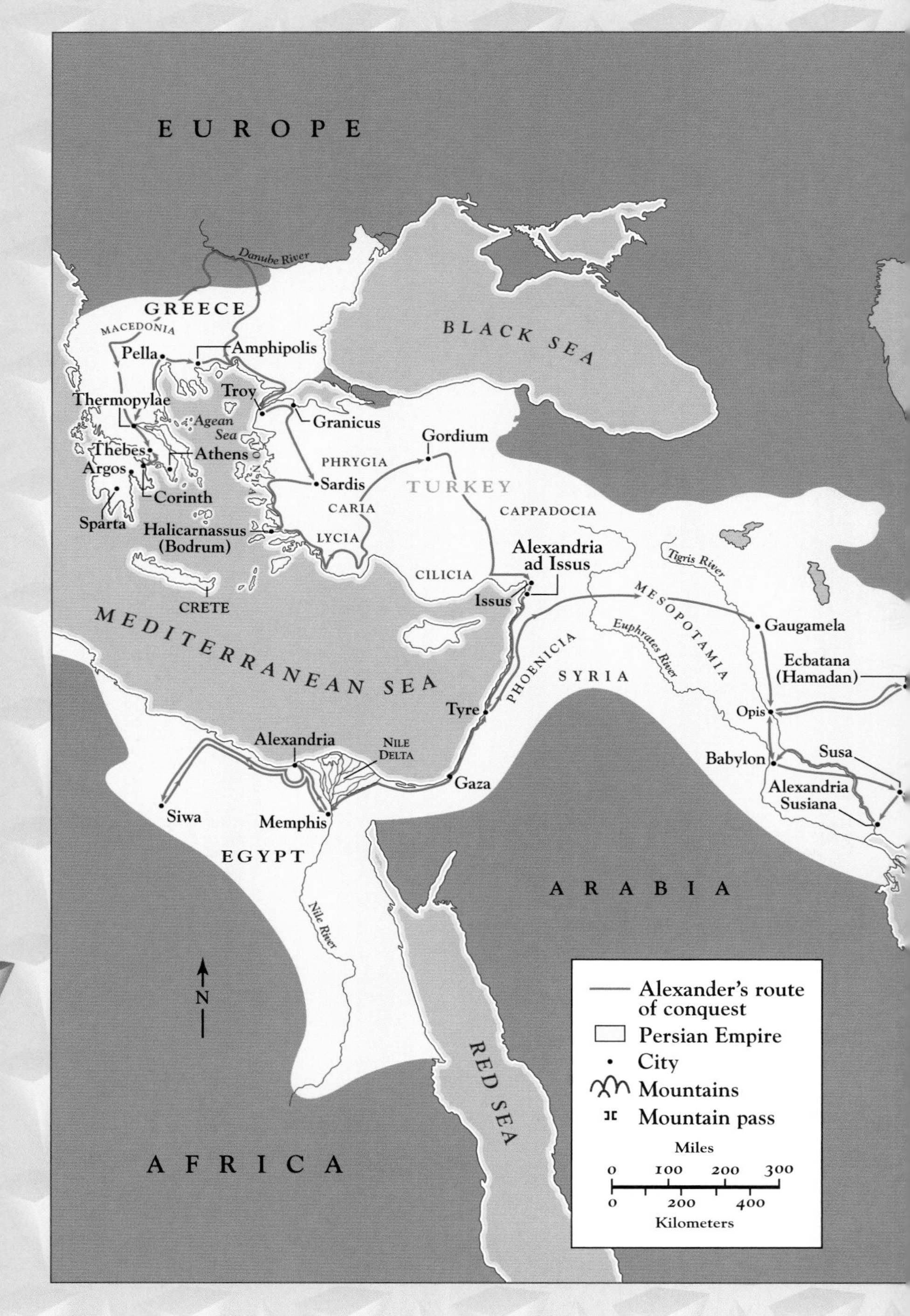

EUROPE
Danube River
GREECE
MACEDONIA
BLACK SEA
Pella
Amphipolis
Troy
Thermopylae
Agean Sea
Granicus
Gordium
Thebes
Athens
PHRYGIA
Argos
Sardis
TURKEY
Corinth
CARIA
CAPPADOCIA
Sparta
Halicarnassus (Bodrum)
LYCIA
Alexandria ad Issus
Tigris River
CILICIA
Issus
MESOPOTAMIA
CRETE
Gaugamela
MEDITERRANEAN SEA
Euphrates River
PHOENICIA
SYRIA
Ecbatana (Hamadan)
Tyre
Opis
Alexandria
NILE DELTA
Babylon
Susa
Gaza
Alexandria Susiana
Siwa
Memphis
EGYPT
ARABIA
Nile River
N
RED SEA
AFRICA
Alexander's route of conquest
Persian Empire
City
Mountains
Mountain pass
Miles
0
100
200
300
0
200
400
Kilometers

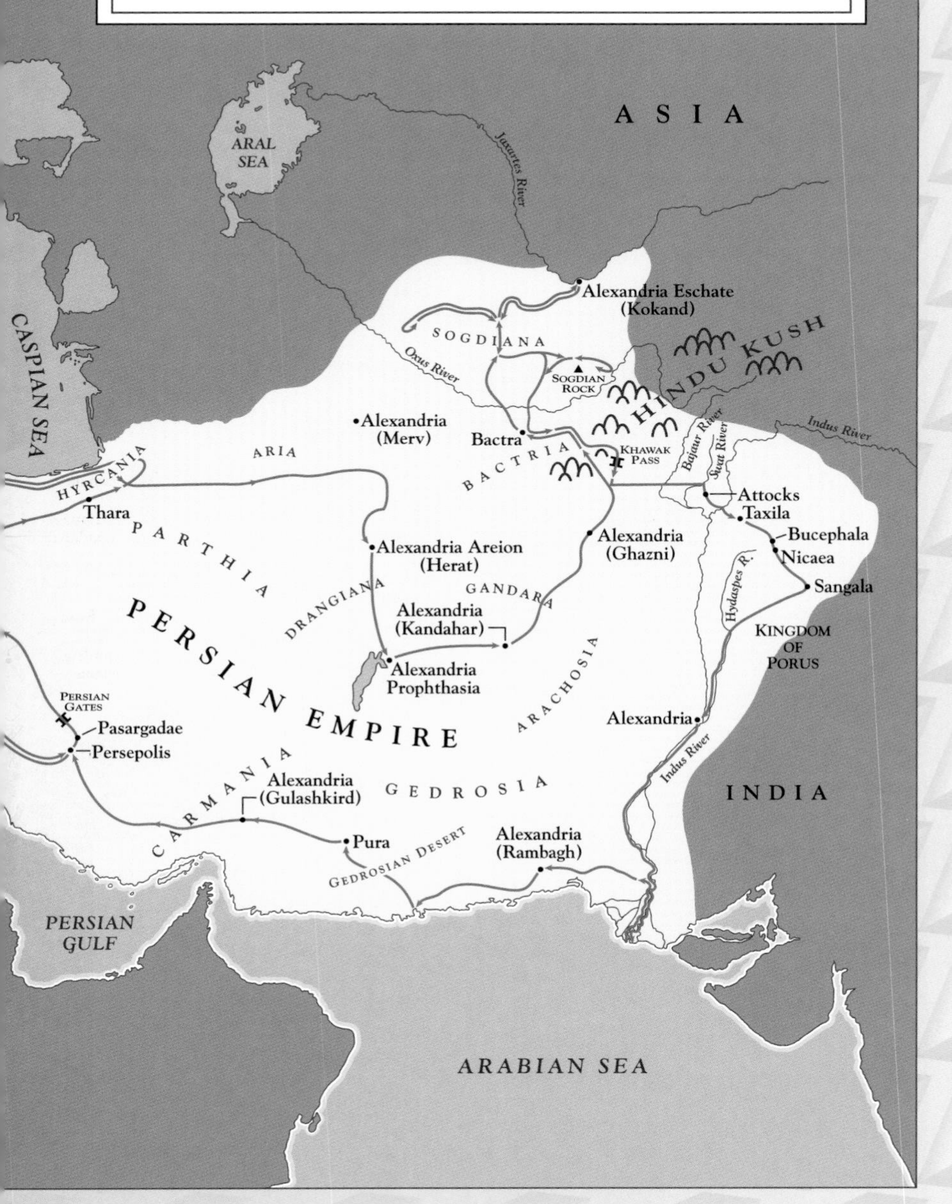
The Conquests of Alexander the Great
334 B.C.–324 B.C.
ASIA
ARAL SEA
Jaxartes River
CASPIAN SEA
Alexandria Eschate (Kokand)
SOGDIANA
Oxus River
SOGDIAN ROCK
HINDU KUSH
Alexandria (Merv)
Bactra
BACTRIA
KHAWAK PASS
Bajaur River
Swat River
Indus River
ARIA
HYRCANIA
Thara
PARTHIA
Attocks
Taxila
Bucephala
Nicaea
Sangala
Alexandria Areion (Herat)
Alexandria (Ghazni)
DRANGIANA
GANDARA
Alexandria (Kandahar)
Hydaspes R.
KINGDOM OF PORUS
PERSIAN EMPIRE
Alexandria Prophthasia
ARACHOSIA
PERSIAN GATES
Pasargadae
Persepolis
Alexandria
Indus River
CARMANIA
Alexandria (Gulashkird)
GEDROSIA
INDIA
Pura
GEDROSIAN DESERT
Alexandria (Rambagh)
PERSIAN GULF
ARABIAN SEA

EPILOGUE
LEGACY

> The great King with his unparalleled worldly success, the undisputed monarch of two continents . . . spread the power of his name over all the earth. . . . [T]here was in those days no nation, no city, no single individual beyond the reach of Alexander's name; never in all the world was there another like him.
>
> —*Arrian, in* The Campaigns of Alexander, ca. A.D. 150

The precise cause of Alexander's death was a mystery—and remains one. At first, accusations of poisoning swirled through the army, but no proof was ever found of such a crime. Other possibilities include an attack of malaria, typhoid, or some other tropical disease, possibly contracted in India's damp heat. Some historians, both ancient and modern, believe that Alexander died as a result of alcoholism, while still others theorize that his battle wounds, combined with the exhaustion of commanding an army for twelve years across thousands of miles, had simply taken their toll on his body.

THE KINGDOM'S FATE

Alexander's vision of a vast and united empire died not long after he did. His force, personality, and charisma had, it seemed, been the main things holding the realm together. For, while unrest had been stirring throughout the empire before his death, it erupted soon afterward. Thousands of Greek mercenaries, no longer willing to fight for Macedonia, revolted. Rebellion also broke out among Persian satraps and Greek city-states.

With no obvious successor, Alexander's officials were left struggling to maintain control. The officials—who became known as the Diadochi, or successors—planned to divide the kingdom among themselves. But these leaders began fighting each other almost immediately, in what were called

AN UNLUCKY HEIR

Very soon after Alexander's death, Roxana gave birth to a son. Named Alexander IV, he was technically the kingdom's heir. But with powerful generals fighting for control, the boy would never see the throne. During the Wars of the Diadochi (322–281 B.C.), Alexander IV and his mother were arrested, imprisoned, and eventually killed in 310 B.C. or 309 B.C.

the Wars of the Diadochi. Erupting in 322 B.C., they lasted more than forty years, finally ending in 281 B.C. By that time, the kingdom had been hacked to pieces and Alexander's original generals were dead. But three families, descended from three of Alexander's lesser commanders, lived on. Ptolemy's heirs held Egypt, the family of Seleucus ruled over Syria and much of Persia, and the descendants of Antigonus controlled most of the Greek mainland.

THE HELLENISTIC AGE

Although Alexander's empire disintegrated, his conquests left a deep and lasting legacy. The Persian Empire had been dismembered, and it would never recover its old power or strength. In addition, as the first European to conquer large parts of Asia, Alexander opened the eyes of many ancient Greeks to a much wider world. The scientists, philosophers, and other experts he had taken on his travels and explorations brought Greece a wealth of new information about the lands to the east. Many soldiers had Persian wives and children, and these new families blended Greek and Persian culture.

The center of the Greek and Mediterranean world was no longer firmly located on the Greek mainland. Instead, it shifted southeastward. The Egyptian city of Alexandria and the Syrian city of Antioch became new hubs of trade, culture, and government. Many Greeks—mostly retired soldiers and their families—had already settled throughout the empire. More Greeks emigrated to these cities, and the power of the old city-states started to decline. At the same

MEASURING UP

Alexander's accomplishments can be measured by many yardsticks. He traveled more than 20,000 miles (32,000 km) in a span of about eleven years. He left the mild Mediterranean climate for the arid deserts of Egypt, Iraq, and Iran; the ancient mountains and plains of Afghanistan; and the tropical heat of India. And he ruled—however briefly—over millions of human beings, who came from dozens of countries, cultures, and religions. He also founded many Alexandrias. In addition to his great port city in Egypt, at least a dozen—and some sources say as many as seventy—other cities sprang up in his wake, from Turkey to Afghanistan. Some were built new, while others were founded on older cities that had been destroyed in the conquests. Rebuilt and renamed, they, too, became Alexandrias. The exact sites of many of these cities have never been found.

time, Alexander's victories sparked an ever greater distribution of Greek culture.

This new trend—the spread of Greek ways, combined with Persian influence on Greece itself—is usually called Hellenism. The families of Ptolemy, Seleucus, and Antigonus, which were still powerful, aided Hellenism's rise. For example, Ptolemy and his descendants, known as the Ptolemaic dynasties, ruled Egypt for nearly three centuries, instilling Greek ideas of government and economics there. The Seleucid dynasty would do the same in Syria and Persia, leaving behind very tangible evidence—coins minted by the

This silver coin bearing Alexander's image was minted in Susa during the reign of Seleucus I, who ruled Seleucid Persia during the late fourth century and early third century B.C.

Seleucids, bearing Alexander's image, have been found as far east as Afghanistan.

Even after the last of the Diadochi lost power, hints of Hellenism lived on far to the east of the Mediterranean. The Greco-Bactrian Kingdom, in modern Afghanistan, lasted until 125 B.C. The Indo-Greek Kingdom was even more powerful, holding a large region in northwestern India and southeastern Pakistan for nearly three hundred years. The rulers of this realm combined Greek culture and symbolism with the customs and religions of the East, including Buddhism and Hinduism. It survived as late as A.D. 10.

A STRING OF EMPIRES

The effects of Alexander's conquests did not end even with the close of the Hellenistic Age. Rulers of the Roman Empire would build on the idea of striking eastward and spreading their culture. This realm arose on the Italian peninsula about one hundred years after Alexander's death. It would eventually envelop Greece and then go on to seize lands throughout Europe, Asia, and Africa. At its height, the empire reached as far east as the Persian Gulf and extended southward to include much of North Africa, including Egypt. And Roman military commanders—leading an army renowned for its organization and strength—used some of Alexander's battle strategies as inspiration for their own.

In the A.D. 600s, the Islamic Empire would change the direction of such imperialism (the creation of an empire). Founded on the Arabian Peninsula and moving westward, this realm's armies launched invasions into Europe from Asia. The Islamic Empire would eventually stretch from Saudi Arabia to Spain.

The tables turned again with the Crusades. This series of wars between 1096 and 1270 was led by European Christians striving to claim the "Holy Land" (comprising modern-day Israel, the Palestinian territories, and surrounding lands) from its Muslim rulers. But Muslim leaders took the upper hand again in the 1300s, founding the powerful Ottoman Empire. This realm, centered in Turkey, reached its peak during the 1500s and 1600s, when it included large portions of the Middle East and North Africa, as well as territory as far west as Hungary.

As the Ottoman Empire began to crumble in the 1800s, the British Empire reached its peak. Based in Great Britain, British armies had created a huge empire that included colonies in Africa, Southeast Asia, the Americas, and Australia. Their greatest prize of all, sometimes known as the "Jewel of the British Empire," was India—Alexander's own great prize.

"ALL THINGS TO ALL MEN"

The final impact and importance of Alexander the Great's conquests is almost inseparable from the legend of the man himself. Biographer Peter Green wrote that, in Alexander's own time, he tried to be "all things to all men." But, as is true of all historical figures—and most especially those from the very distant past—Alexander has been judged by each generation according to the views and values of the time and place. During the height of British colonialism in the 1800s, many Europeans regarded Alexander as an intrepid pioneer. But in the years following World War II (1939–1945), after the world had seen the horrors committed by German dictator Adolf Hitler, opinion changed. Alexander was condemned as an egomaniac bent on world domination. Similarly, modern Macedonians consider him a hometown hero, while present-day Zoroastrians have little fondness for the man who destroyed the Persian Empire.

Alexander's deeds even touch on facets of modern life. Some of his most brilliant military maneuvers are still studied, while modern businesspeople look to him for timeless lessons in leadership and success. Dozens of travel agencies offer tours that follow "the footsteps of Alexander the Great." Two major motion pictures were made about his life in the first decade of the twenty-first century. It seems that this man and his deeds, as mysterious as many of the details may be, are simply too intriguing to be ignored, even more than two thousand years after his death.

Many mysteries do remain. Was his adoption of Persian culture truly tolerant, or merely the move of a shrewd politician? Did he leave Macedonia in search of glory, revenge, or simply adventure? And was he driven onward to further conquests by ego and selfish ambition, by an urge to spread the culture of Greece, or by a bolder, purer vision for a new kind of empire? We will never know for sure. Alexander's mystery—combined with the indelible mark he left on the world—is part of his enduring fascination.

His conquests led, in part, to centuries of competition and warfare between the "West" (usually defined as Western Europe and North America) and the "East" (Asia), which in turn left deep and lingering tensions. Even in the twenty-first century, relations between Western and non-Western nations are often troubled. At the same time, communication and interaction among very different cultures has never been greater. In the end, throwing open the doors between peoples, nations, and religions—allowing for the freer exchange of knowledge and ideas—may be the best legacy of Alexander the Great's conquests. From a kingdom too small for his ambitions, he created a legend larger than life.

PRIMARY SOURCE RESEARCH

To learn about historical events, people study many sources, such as books, websites, newspaper articles, photographs, and paintings. These sources can be separated into two general categories—primary sources and secondary sources.

A primary source is the record of an eyewitness. Primary sources provide firsthand accounts about a person or event. Examples include diaries, letters, autobiographies, speeches, newspapers, and oral history interviews. Libraries, archives, historical societies, and museums often have primary sources available on-site or on the Internet.

A secondary source is published information that was researched, collected, and written or otherwise created by someone who was not an eyewitness. These authors or artists use primary sources and other secondary sources in their research, but they interpret and arrange the source material in their own works. Secondary sources include history books, novels, biographies, movies, documentaries, and magazines. Libraries and museums are filled with secondary sources.

After finding primary and secondary sources, authors and historians must evaluate them. They may ask questions such as: Who created this document? What is this person's point of view? What biases might this person have? How trustworthy is this document? Just because a person was an eyewitness to an event does not mean that person recorded the whole truth about that event. For example, a soldier describing a battle might depict only the heroic actions of his unit and only the brutal behavior of the enemy. An account from a soldier on the opposing side might portray the same battle very differently. When sources disagree, researchers must decide through additional study which explanation makes the most sense. For this reason, historians consult a variety of primary and secondary sources. Then they can draw their own conclusions.

The Pivotal Moments in History series takes readers on a journey to the important junctures in history that shaped our modern world. Authors researched each event using both primary and secondary sources, an approach that enhances readers' awareness of the complexities of the materials and rich stories from which we draw our understanding of our shared history.

STUDYING ALEXANDER THE GREAT

People who study and write about Alexander the Great and his conquests face several challenges. To begin with, all written primary sources directly regarding Alexander—such as journals kept by his soldiers or records kept by his officials—have been lost. However, we do have secondary sources—ancient themselves—to draw upon. The writers of these works used earlier primary sources before they disappeared. In turn, other writings drew upon those secondary sources, and so forth.

All of this writing and study over the centuries means that there is no shortage of resources on Alexander. But with each level that removes us further from the original sources, new room opens up for error, bias, and confusion to sneak in. And when ancient texts written in Greek and Latin are translated into English and other languages, this translation offers yet another opportunity for distortion and inaccuracies.

Written works are not the only type of primary source. Many statues of Alexander were made in his lifetime—but, like writings, these figures have been lost over the centuries. Only copies remain. In addition, coins minted throughout his empire are struck with his likeness, offering a glimpse of the young general's profile. However, these were mostly made after his death. Some of the cities that Alexander founded during his conquests remain, and even these are primary sources, in a way. But they have been changed greatly by time.

Even in Alexander's own day, many accounts of his deeds were unreliable. In many ways, Alexander was one of the world's first great celebrities. He was young, brilliant, accomplished, and wealthy. He was also moody, stubborn, and very, very sure of himself. As a result, he inspired adoration, jealousy, praise, and plenty of gossip. And, like modern celebrities, Alexander was a media star. As tales of his adventures spread across the ancient world, they were probably frequently exaggerated. Some authors, dazzled by the young king's power and wealth, may have written adoring but insincere praise in hopes of being rewarded. Likewise, especially harsh critics might have been blinded by jealousy or resentment. For every person who spoke or wrote in glowing terms of the charismatic young general, another dwelled on his supposed flaws. Some called him rash rather than bold, foolish instead of inspired. He was alternately described as merciful and bloodthirsty, modest and arrogant.

Not surprisingly then, the ancient secondary sources often disagree on the events of Alexander's life and conquests, especially when it comes to details. Arrian, a Greek scholar who lived in the first century A.D., is seen by historians as one of the most reliable sources. But Arrian himself confesses at the opening of his *Campaigns of Alexander*, "there are other accounts of Alexander's life—more of them, indeed, and more mutually conflicting than of any other historical character." Other important historical sources include Diodorus Siculus (a Sicilian who wrote in the first century B.C.), and the first-century A.D. Greek Plutarch and Roman Quintus Curtius Rufus. They provide valuable information, but all of them lived centuries after Alexander's death.

For all of these reasons, each new author who chooses Alexander as a subject has to make his or her own decisions about the most likely "truth"—although we will probably never know for certain. And no matter how hard writers try to make the best decisions they can, their choices inevitably reflect their own feelings and opinions. In the end, each reader must draw his or her own conclusions about an author's reliability and about the truth or falsehood of any given story.

However, even when primary sources—or even reliable secondary sources—are in short supply, a variety of other tools can be helpful. For example, historians can draw some conclusions about Alexander based on the things that he read and studied himself. For example, as a boy, Alexander's tutor was the philosopher Aristotle. So Aristotle's own works and teachings may shed some light on Alexander's view of the world. Alexander was also said to have quoted frequently from the works of Euripides (485–406 B.C.), his favorite playwright, and he loved *The Iliad*, a classic work by the poet Homer.

And Alexander, like most young men in the ancient Greek world, knew well the tales of the region's most important historical events, such as the Persian Wars (490–479 B.C.) and the Peloponnesian War (431–404 B.C.). Writers such as Herodotus, Xenophon, Thucydides, and Josephus had spread the stories of these conflicts' battles and heroes. While these records may not tell us about the battles Alexander himself fought, they can shed some light on his character by revealing the influences that may have affected him. Even information about what life was like in the ancient Greek world where Alexander was raised, as well as in the Asian lands that he conquered, can be useful. Ancient Greek and Persian art depicting families, homes, meals, celebrations, and more can give us glimpses of what it might have been like to live in the age of Alexander. All of this background offers insight, not only into Alexander's own character, but also into how deeply his deeds changed the lives of ancient Greeks and Persians, and far beyond—even up to our own time.

PRIMARY SOURCE COINS

One of the questions that historians have tried to answer is what Alexander looked like. Although many statues and other artistic depictions of him exist, nearly all were made after his death. Plutarch states that "The best likeness of Alexander which has been preserved for us is . . . the statues sculpted by Lysippus, the only artist whom Alexander considered worthy to represent him. Alexander possessed . . . a poise of the neck which was tilted slightly to the left, or a certain melting look in his eyes. . . . [W]e are told that he was fair-skinned, with a ruddy tinge that showed itself especially upon his face and chest." Aelian, a Roman author of the A.D. 100s–200s, wrote, "They say that Alexander . . . enjoyed natural good looks, with curly, fair hair, but they add that there was something in his appearance which aroused fear." In addition to these descriptions, a number of stories suggest that Alexander was of relatively small stature.

However, we have only one image of Alexander that historians widely believe was made during his lifetime. This portrait appears on an ancient silver coin. The coin is estimated to have been created in approximately 324 B.C., following Alexander's victory over the Indian leader Porus. Now housed at the British Museum, this precious artifact may be one of very few primary sources offering a visual depiction of the ancient Macedonian king and general. Looking at it closely offers several important clues that it does, indeed, show Alexander the Great.

On one side of the coin, we see a human figure—probably Alexander himself. He stands upright, wearing what experts have identified as a Macedonian cloak, Greek armor, and a Persian headdress. The combination of these garments may represent Alexander's ethnic and political heritage blending with the cultures he conquered.

The figure on this side of the coin also grasps a thunderbolt in one hand. In ancient Greek religion, the god Zeus controlled thunder and lightning, so this detail could be intended to show that the figure is divine. Many stories were told of Alexander's possible family connections to the gods, and the ambitious king did not always silence such tales. So this depiction may have been intended to add strength to these ideas of his divinity.

This coin is believed to be the only image of Alexander made during his lifetime.

On the coin's opposite side, we see another image that is also believed to be of Alexander. In this scene, a figure on horseback attacks a foe who is sitting on top of an elephant. This depiction probably represents Alexander in combat with Porus during the Battle of the Hydaspes in 326 B.C. The coin itself was likely created to celebrate that momentous victory.

We still don't know beyond the shadow of a doubt that this worn, centuries-old coin is a primary source from the days of Alexander. But by carefully examining the evidence and drawing conclusions based on our observations, we can make an educated guess. And these conclusions can, in turn, tell us even more about this larger-than-life king and general, Alexander the Great.

The reverse of the coin shows Alexander in battle.

TIMELINE

559 B.C.	Persian ruler Cyrus the Great takes power.
499–480	The Persian Wars
CA. 479	The Classical Period of Greece begins.
431–404	The Peloponnesian War
359	King Philip II becomes Macedonia's ruler.
358	Artaxerxes III seizes the Persian throne in a bloody coup.
356	Alexander III of Macedon is born to Philip and his wife, Queen Olympias.
338	Alexander joins his father on the battlefield.
336	Philip is murdered. Alexander becomes king. In Persia, Darius III takes the throne.
335	Alexander's army lays siege to the Greek city of Thebes.
334	Alexander and his army leave for Asia in the spring. The Battle of the Granicus takes place in spring. In summer Alexander's troops begin a months-long siege of Halicarnassus.
333	Alexander reaches Gordium in the spring. In fall, he defeats Darius at the Battle of Issus.

332	Alexander's army reaches Tyre early in the year and lays siege to the city. The siege ends in the summer. Alexander reaches Egypt in late fall.
331	Alexander heads east toward Persia in midsummer. That autumn, his army clashes with that of Darius at the Battle of Gaugamela. The army encamps at Babylon before moving on to Susa at year's end.
330	Alexander and the army reach Persepolis early in the year, pillaging and burning parts of the great city. In early summer, he begins a swift pursuit of Bessus and Darius. Bessus murders Darius in midsummer. That autumn, the army reaches the Caspian Sea.
329	Alexander leads the army in a grueling march across the Hindu Kush in the early spring. They reach the Oxus River weeks later and capture Bessus. That summer and fall, the army begins more than a year of campaigns in Sogdiana and Bactria.
328	In the autumn, Alexander kills Cleitus. The Persian general Spitamenes dies that winter.
327	Alexander and his men capture Sogdian Rock early in the year. That summer, Alexander and Roxana, the daughter of Oxyartes, are wed. In the autumn, the army splits up to subdue regions east of Bactria and in the Bajaur and Swat river valleys.

326	Alexander and the army reach the Indus River in the spring. Alexander defeats the Indian raja Porus at the Battle of the Hydaspes. Bucephalus dies and is honored with a grand funeral. The troops mutiny in the summer, and Alexander agrees to head homeward. They begin moving down the Indus in late fall.
325	Alexander divides the army again in summer, sending Craterus and troops west to Arachosia and continuing with the rest of the army to what he believes is the Great Ocean. When they reach the water, Alexander leads troops on a brutal and costly march across the deserts of Carmania and Gedrosia.
324	The army is reunited. They reach Susa in the spring and Alexander holds a mass wedding celebration for dozens of his men and their Persian brides. In late summer, a second mutiny erupts. Hephaestion dies that autumn. Alexander arranges lavish funeral honors.
323	Alexander and the army arrive in Babylon in early spring. Alexander falls ill suddenly in the spring. A few weeks later, Alexander the Great dies. Roxana gives birth to a son, Alexander IV, shortly afterward.
322	The Wars of the Diadochi erupt. The Age of Hellenism begins.

310 OR 309	Roxana and Alexander IV are killed.
281	The Wars of the Diadochi end.
125	The Greco-Bactrian Kingdom, which grew out of Alexander's conquests in Afghanistan, falls.
CA. A.D. 10	The Indo-Greek Kingdom ends.
600s	The Islamic Empire rises.
1096–1270	The Crusades take place.
1300s	The Ottoman Empire is formed.
1600s	The British East India Company is formed and begins establishing trading posts and other territory on the Indian subcontinent. This leads to the rise of the British Empire.
1798–1799	French general and emperor Napoleon invades Egypt.
1800s	The Ottoman Empire weakens, and the British Empire flourishes.

GLOSSARY

AGRIANIANS: javelin throwers in the Greek army

ARAMAIC: an ancient language of southwest Asia

ATHANATOI (IMMORTALS): elite unit of the Persian army

BAIVARABA: Persian army divisions of ten thousand soldiers

BARBARIANS: inferior foreigners. The Greeks considered most foreigners barbarians.

BEL-MARDUK: the supreme Babylonian god

CHILIARCHIES: thousand-man units of the Greek army

CONCUBINE: a woman of the household who is not a legally accepted wife

CUNEIFORM: an ancient wedge-shaped form of writing usually impressed into clay or carved into stone

HAZARABA: thousand-man units of the Persian army

HELLENISM: the Persian-influenced Greek culture that took hold after Alexander's death

HELLESPONT: a narrow waterway in present-day Turkey that marks the official crossing from Europe into Asia

HETAIROI: a Greek cavalry unit that carried heavy weapons, such as spears and swords

LEAGUE OF CORINTH: an alliance between Macedonia and most of the Greek city-states that lasted from 337 B.C. to 323 B.C.

MEDIAN: the language of the Medes, early people of Persia

MERCENARIES: hired soldiers

MYRIADS: Greek army divisions of ten thousand soldiers

OLD PERSIAN: an ancient form of the modern-day language, Farsi, spoken in Iran

OLIGARCHY: a government ruled by a small group of powerful people

PHALANGITES: members of a phalanx

PHALANX: a tight military formation of infantry. Members of ancient Greek phalanxes carried a double-pointed pike.

POLIS: a Greek city-state. Some of the most powerful city-states controlled thousands of square miles.

POLYGAMOUS: having many wives

PRODROMOI: an ancient Greek cavalry unit that carried light spears and javelins

PROSKYNESIS: the Persian custom of showing honor to superiors through ritualistic bowing and kissing

RAJA: a king, or regional ruler, in India

Bagoas crowned Codomannus, who took the name Darius III as king. But Darius resisted Bagoas's attempts to control and later to kill him. Darius had his hands full running the vast Persian Empire, and although he tried to defend it against Alexander's attacks, he ultimately failed. He was defeated by the Macedonians in battle and finally assassinated by the ambitious satrap Bessus.

HEPHAESTION (CA. 356–324 B.C.) The son of a wealthy Macedonian family, Hephaestion probably met Alexander when both of them were students. They may have even studied together under Aristotle. The two grew to be close friends as youths and remained so throughout life. As a member of the Macedonian army's prized Companion Cavalry, Hephaestion accompanied Alexander when he began his expedition to Asia in 334. Despite the fact that many other Macedonian military leaders saw him as woefully unqualified, Hephaestion went on to become a top-ranking officer. He was also Alexander's closest and most trusted adviser and was believed by many to have been the king's romantic companion. In the autumn of 324, Hephaestion suddenly fell ill and died. Alexander honored his fallen friend and general with a lavish state funeral.

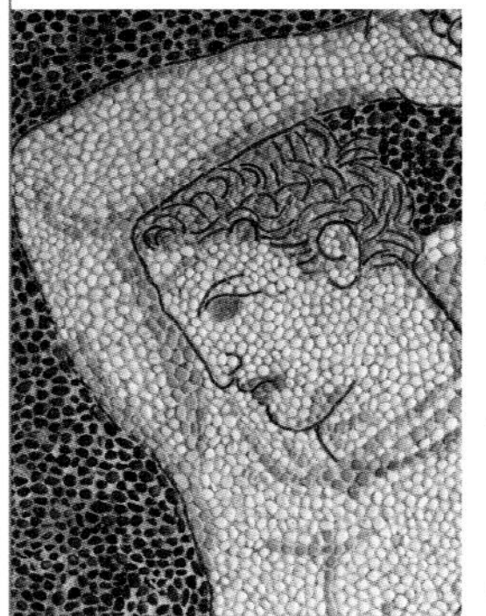

OLYMPIAS OF MACEDON (CA. 376–316 B.C.) Born in the Greek region of Epirus, Princess Olympias was married off to King Philip II of Macedon in 359 for political reasons. But while her marriage to Philip was not ideal, Olympias treasured the son they had together—Alexander. After Philip took a second wife in about 337, Olympias remained close to Alexander. She was even rumored to have played a role in Philip's assassination, in order to guarantee that Alexander would become king. She remained an influential—and sometimes ruthless—leader in Macedonia while Alexander led the army through Asia and even after her son's death.

PARMENIO (CA. 400–330 B.C.) The son of Macedonian nobleman Philotas, Parmenio served as a general to both King Philip II and to Alexander the Great. Often described by historians as a skillful and prudent commander, Parmenio led parts of Alexander's army in many major battles throughout Asia. But in about 330 B.C., rumors surfaced that Parmenio's son Philotas was involved in a plot to murder Alexander. To extinguish the threat Alexander ordered first the execution of Philotas and then that of his old comrade Parmenio.

PHILIP II OF MACEDON (382–336 B.C.) Alexander's father, Philip, took the Macedonian throne in 359 B.C. He swiftly began making changes to the kingdom's army, and he set out to subdue unrest in Macedonia and to conquer

new territory beyond. Both a talented military commander and a skillful politician, Philip soon made his little kingdom a force to be reckoned with. And he made certain that his son, Alexander, gained experience in war and governance. But in about 337 B.C., when Philip took a second wife, Alexander's future was far from certain. Only about a year later, the king was assassinated. The killer was never identified, and the motive was never absolutely clear. Nevertheless, Alexander took the throne in 336 B.C.

PORUS (?–BETWEEN 321 AND 315 B.C.) Few details exist describing the life of Porus. Historians do know that he was a raja, or Indian leader, who ruled over a region near the modern region of Punjab. When Alexander the Great invaded the realm, Porus fought back so fiercely and steadfastly that Alexander himself was impressed by the raja's bravery. Even after Porus was defeated by the Macedonians at the Battle of the Hydaspes in 326 B.C., he retained his dignity. He may have gone on to be a ruler within Alexander's kingdom. A few years later, however, Porus was killed by Greek assassins in the chaos after Alexander's death.

PTOLEMY I SOTER (367–283 B.C.) One of Alexander's top generals, Ptolemy was rumored to be Alexander's half brother. His mother, a Macedonian beauty, was at one time a lover of King Philip II. Ptolemy was a friend of

Alexander's and, eventually, one of his highest-ranking military commanders. He became the Egyptian satrap after Alexander's death and had to defend his realm fiercely in the Wars of the Diadochi. His descendants ruled Egypt for almost three hundred years. Ptolemy wrote an account of his time in Alexander's army and founded a great library at Alexandria.

ROXANA (SOMETIME BEFORE 341–310 OR 309 B.C.) Roxana was the daughter of Oxyartes, a powerful Bactrian military commander and leader. Following Alexander's surprise capture of the Sogdian Rock, defended by Oxyartes, the Macedonian king asked that Roxana be his wife. Oxyartes agreed, and Roxana and Alexander were married in 327 B.C. But the bride soon became a widow when Alexander died in 323 B.C. Soon afterward she gave birth to a son named Alexander IV. Then, as the fight over Alexander's empire raged, Roxana and her young son—heir to the throne—found their lives in great danger. They were arrested and eventually executed.

SELEUCUS I NICATOR (CA. 358–281 B.C.) Seleucus became one of Alexander's top generals and joined him on his Asian campaigns, and gained power over the Babylonian satrapy. In the Wars of the Diadochi, Seleucus laid the foundation for the Seleucid dynasty. He built a capital on the Tigris River, and although he was assassinated by a relative of Ptolemy I in 281, his heirs ruled over Syria and Persia for several generations more.

SOURCE NOTES

4 Plutarch, "On the Fortune or the Virtue of Alexander," *Lacus Curtius*, n.d., http://penelope.uchicago.edu/Thayer/E/Roman/Texts/Plutarch/Moralia/Fortuna_Alexandri*/2.html (January 25, 2006).

5 Plutarch, *The Age of Alexander*, trans. Ian Scott-Kilvert. (New York: Penguin Books, 1982), 258.

10 Aristotle, *Politics*, trans. Benjamin Jowettt. (Mineola, NY: Dover Publications, Inc., 2000), 106.

12 "Homeric Hymns," *The Perseus Digital Library*, ed. Hugh G. Evelyn-White. n.d., http://www.perseus.tufts.edu/cgi-bin/ptext?doc=Perseus%3Atext%3A1999.01.0138 (January 25, 2006).

17 Homer, *The Odyssey*, trans. Robert Fagles. (New York: Penguin Books, 1997), 77.

19 Herodotus, *The Histories*, trans. Aubrey de Sélincourt. (New York: Penguin Books, 2003), 517.

22 Plutarch, *Age of Alexander*, 256.

25 Ibid.

25 Diodorus, *Library of History: Books XVI.66–XVII*, 79.

25 Ibid.

28 Ibid., 125.

29 Arrian, *The Campaigns of Alexander*, trans. Aubrey de Sélincourt. (New York: Penguin Books, 1971), 59.

34 Quintus Curtius Rufus, *The History of Alexander*, trans. John Yardley. (New York: Penguin Books, 2001), 46.

34 Ibid.

35 Diodorus, *Library of History: Books XVI.66–XVII*, 163.

36 Homer, *The Iliad*, trans. Robert Fagles. (New York: Penguin Books, 1998), 299.

38 Herodotus, *Histories*, 443–444.

41 Arrian, *Campaigns of Alexander*, 70.

41 Ibid., 72.

46 Diodorus, *Library of History: Books XVI.66–XVII*, 193.

47 Arrian, *Campaigns of Alexander*, 105.

50 Ibid., 211.

51 Rufus, *History of Alexander*, 51.

51 Ibid.

52 Plutarch, *Age of Alexander*, 279.

52–53 Ibid.

57 Plutarch, *Age of Alexander*, 283.

57 Quintus Curtius Rufus, *History of Alexander*, 68.

58 Jona Lendering, "Darius the Great: Building Inscription from Persepolis," *Livius: Articles on Ancient History*, 2006, http://www.livius.org/da-dd/darius/darius_i_t10.html (January 26, 2006).

62 Shapour Suren-Pahlav, ed., "History of Iran: Cyrus Charter of Human Rights," *Iran Chamber*, n.d., http://www.iranchamber.com/history/cyrus/cyrus_charter/php (January 5, 2007).

63 Herodotus, "On the Customs of the Persians, c. 430 BCE," *Internet Ancient History Sourcebook*, n.d., http://www.fordham.edu/halsall/ancient/herodotus-persians.html (January 25, 2006).

64 Jona Lendering, "Achaemenid Royal Inscriptions: XPh ('Daiva Inscription')," *Livius: Articles on Ancient History*, 2006, http://www.livius.org/aa-ac/achaemenians/XPh.html (January 26, 2006).

70 Rufus, *History of Alexander*, 77.

72 Plutarch, *Age of Alexander*, 288.

72 Ibid.

72 Ibid., 288–289.

74–75 Arrian, *Campaigns of Alexander*, 170–171.

75 Ibid., 173.

75 Rufus, *History of Alexander*, 93.

76 Diodorus, *Library of History: Books XVI.66–XVII*, 301.

78 Jona Lendering, "Susa," *Livius: Articles on Ancient History*, 2006, http://www.livius.org/su-sz/susa/susa.htm (January 26, 2006).

78 Ibid., 305.

79–80 Rufus, *History of Alexander*, 101.

80 Arrian, *Campaigns of Alexander*, 178.

80 Marcus Junianus Justinus,"Epitome of the Philippic History of Pompeius Trogus, Book 11," *Corpus Scriptorum Latinorum: A Digital Library of Latin Literature*, 2003, http://www.forumromanum.org/literature/justin/english/trans11.html (January 26, 2006).

81 Rufus, *History of Alexander*, 107.

82 Plutarch, *Age of Alexander*, 300.

82 Ibid.

84 Plutarch, *Age of Alexander*, 301.

85 Rufus, *History of Alexander*, 121–122.

87 Plutarch, *Age of Alexander*, 303.

88 Arrian, *Campaigns of Alexander*, 293.

91 Ibid., 195.

94 Ibid., 214.

94 Plutarch, *Age of Alexander*, 309.

95 Rufus, *History of Alexander*, 107.

95 Plutarch, *Age of Alexander*, 277.

96 Arrian, *Campaigns of Alexander*, 234.

97 Rufus, *History of Alexander*, 186.

99 Ibid., 198.

100 Arrian, *Campaigns of Alexander*, 253.

101 Rufus, *History of Alexander*, 205.

101–102 Ibid.

103 Arrian, *Campaigns of Alexander*, 278.

103 Ibid.

104 Ibid., 280.

105 Ibid., 282.

105 Plutarch, *Age of Alexander*, 319.

105 Arrian, *Campaigns of Alexander*, 291.

106 Ibid.

107 Rufus, *History of Alexander*, 218.

107 Arrian, *Campaigns of Alexander*, 298.

107 Ibid.

108 Diodorus, *Library of History: Books XVI.66–XVII*, 413.

108 Arrian, *Campaigns of Alexander*, 319.

109 Waldemar Heckel and J. C. Yardley, ed., *Alexander the Great: Historical Sources in Translation* (Malden, MA: Blackwell Publishing, 2004), 262.

112 Arrian, *Campaigns of Alexander*, 360.

112 Ibid., 354.

114 Ibid., 364.

114 Ibid., 365.

114 Ibid., 365–366.

114 Rufus, *History of Alexander*, 46.

115 Diodorus, *Library of History: Books XVI.66–XVII*, 455.

115 Ibid., 451.

116 Ibid., 467.

116 Euripedes, *The Bacchae*, tr. William Arrowsmith, in *Greek Tragedies: Volume 3*, eds. David Grene and Richard Lattimore (Chicago: University of Chicago Press, 1972), 193–194.

117 Arrian, *Campaigns of Alexander*, 393.

117 Ibid.

117 Heckel and Yardley, *Alexander the Great: Historical Sources in Translation*, 277.

117 Arrian, *Campaigns of Alexander*, 394.

117 Rufus, *History of Alexander*, 246.

120 Arrian, *Campaigns of Alexander*, 398.

126 Peter Green, *Alexander of Macedon, 356–323* B.C.*:* A *Historical Biography* (Berkeley: University of California Press, 1991), 368.

131 Arrain, *Campaigns of Alexander*, 41.

133 Plutarch, *Age of Alexander*, 255.

133 Heckel and Yardley, *Alexander the Great: Historical Sources in Translation*, 37.

SELECTED BIBLIOGRAPHY

PRIMARY AND SECONDARY SOURCES

Anonymous. *The Greek Alexander Romance*. Translated by Richard Stoneman. New York: Penguin Books, 1991.

Aristotle. *Politics*. Translated by Aubrey de Sélincourt. Mineola, NY: Dover Publications, Inc., 2000.

Arrian. *The Campaigns of Alexander*. Translated by Aubrey de Sélincourt. New York: Penguin Books, 1971.

Diodorus Siculus. *Library of History: Books XVI.66–XVII*. Translated by C. Bradford Welles. Cambridge, MA: Harvard University Press, 2003.

Heckel, Waldemar, and J. C. Yardley, eds. *Alexander the Great: Historical Sources in Translation*. Malden, MA: Blackwell Publishing, 2004.

Herodotus. *The Histories*. Translated by Aubrey de Sélincourt. New York: Penguin Books, 2003.

———. "On the Customs of the Persians, c. 430 BCE." *Internet Ancient History Sourcebook*. N.d. http://www.fordham.edu/halsall/ancient/herodotus-persians.html (January 25, 2006).

Homer. *The Iliad*. Translated by Robert Fagles. New York: Penguin Books, 1998.

———. *The Odyssey*. Translated by Robert Fagles. New York: Penguin Books, 1997.

Plutarch. *The Age of Alexander*. Translated by Ian Scott-Kilvert. New York: Penguin Books, 1982.

Quintus Curtius Rufus. *The History of Alexander*. Translated by John Yardley. New York: Penguin Books, 2001.

OTHER SOURCES

Cawthorne, Nigel. *Alexander the Great*. London: Haus Publishing Limited, 2004.

de Souza, Philip, Waldemar Heckel, and Lloyd Llewellyn-Jones. *The Greeks at War: From Athens to Alexander*. Oxford, UK: Osprey Publishing, 2004.

Fuller, J. F. C. *The Generalship of Alexander the Great*. New York: Da Capo Press, 1960.

Green, Peter. *Alexander of Macedon, 356–323* B.C.*: A Historical Biography*. Berkeley: University of California Press, 1991.

Halsall, Paul, ed. *Internet Ancient History Sourcebook*. N.d. http://www.fordham.edu/halsall/ancient/asbook.html (July 1, 2005).

Hammond, N. G. L. *The Genius of Alexander the Great*. Chapel Hill: University of North Carolina Press, 1997.

Lendering, Jona. *Livius: Articles on Ancient History*. 2006. http://www.livius.org/home.html (January 26, 2006).

Savill, Agnes. *Alexander the Great and His Time*. New York: Barnes and Noble Books, 1993.

FURTHER READING AND WEBSITES

BOOKS

Adkins, Lesley, and Roy A. Adkins. *Handbook to Life in Ancient Greece*. New York: Facts On File, 2005.

Behnke, Alison. *Afghanistan in Pictures*. Minneapolis: Twenty-First Century Books, 2003.

Graves, Robert. *The Greek Myths*. New York: Penguin Books: 1993.

Homer. *The Iliad*. Trans. Robert Fagles. New York: Penguin Books, 1998.

———. *The Odyssey*. Trans. Robert Fagles. New York: Penguin Books, 1997.

Lane Fox, Robin. *Alexander the Great*. New York: Penguin Books, 1986.

Plutarch. *The Age of Alexander*. Trans. Ian Scott-Kilvert. New York: Penguin Books, 1982.

Quintus Curtius Rufus. *The History of Alexander*. Trans. John Yardley. New York: Penguin Books, 2001.

Taus-Bolstad, Stacy. *Iran in Pictures*. Minneapolis: Twenty-First Century Books, 2004.

———. *Iraq in Pictures*. Minneapolis: Twenty-First Century Books, 2004.

Wood, Michael. *In the Footsteps of Alexander the Great*. Berkeley: University of California Press, 1997.

Woods, Michael, and Mary B. Woods. *Ancient Warfare: From Clubs to Catapults*. Minneapolis: Twenty-First Century Books, 2000.

Zuehlke, Jeffrey. *Egypt in Pictures*. Minneapolis: Twenty-First Century Books, 2003.

WEBSITES

Alexander the Great http://history.boisestate.edu/westciv/alexander/ This biography, written by a professor of history at Boise State University, provides a great overview of Alexander's life. The site also includes clickable sound files offering pronunciation of difficult and unfamiliar terms.

Alexander the Great: Hunting for a New Past http://www.bbc.co.uk/history/ancient/greeks/alexander_the_great_01.shtml In this online article from the BBC's ancient history section, Professor Paul Cartledge examines Alexander's life and the mystery surrounding it.

Alexander the Great on the Web http://www.isidore-of-seville.com/alexander/index.html Visit this site to find dozens of Alexander-related links.

Ancient Warfare http://www.dean.usma.edu/history/atlases/ancient_warfare/ancient_warfare_table_of_contents.html Check out the Alexander the Great section of this site for diagrams of Alexander's greatest battles.

CIA – *The World Factbook: Macedonia* http://www.cia.gov/cia/publications/factbook/geos/mk.html This page offers basic background information and fast facts about modern Macedonia.

In Pictures: Zoroastrians in Iran http://news.bbc.co.uk/2/shared/spl/hi/picture_gallery/05/middle_east_zoroastrians_in_iran/html/1.stm This slide show from BBC News Online presents images of modern Zoroastrians practicing their ancient Persian religion.

Internet Ancient History Sourcebook: Greece http://www.fordham.edu/halsall/ancient/asbook07.html Read full and partial texts from ancient Greek writers at this site.

Internet Ancient History Sourcebook: Persia http://www.fordham.edu/halsall/ancient/asbook05.html Explore ancient Persian writings in this online library.

In the Footsteps of Alexander the Great http://www.mpt.org/programsinterests/mpt/alexander/ This website is a companion to the book and film by Michael Wood, in which Wood travels along Alexander's ancient route through Asia.

INDEX

ABOUT THE AUTHOR

Alison Behnke is an author and editor of books for young readers. Among her many books are *Afghanistan in Pictures*, *Pope John Paul II*, and *Jack Kerouac*. She first learned about Alexander the Great in the third grade, and she has remained fascinated by world history and ancient cultures ever since. She loves to read, write and travel, and she lives in Rome, Italy.

PHOTO ACKNOWLEDGMENTS

The images in this book were used with the permission of: The Art Archive/Chiaramonti Museum Vatican/Dagli Orti, p. 5; The Art Archive/Archaeological Museum Naples/Dagli Orti, p. 6; © Laura Westlund/Independent Picture Service, pp. 8, 39, 59, 89, 118–119; © Getty Images, p. 13; © Gianni Dagli Orti/CORBIS, pp. 18, 86; © Bridgeman Art Library/Getty Images, p. 23; The Art Archive/Musée du Louvre Paris/Dagli Orti, p. 27; © Time Life Pictures/Getty Images, p. 32; The Art Archive/Archaeological Museum Salonica/Dagli Orti, pp. 34, 145; © Christel Gerstenberg/CORBIS, p. 37; Réunion des Musées Nationaux/Art Resource, NY, pp. 43, 53, 74, 104; © SuperStock, Inc./SuperStock, pp. 49, 111; Cameraphoto Arte, Venice/Art Resource, NY, p. 55; © The British Museum/Topham-HIP/The Image Works, p. 61; The Art Archive/Dagli Orti, p. 67; The Art Archive/Archaeological Museum Teheran/Dagli Orti, p. 68; The Art Archive/Bibliothéque Municipale Reims/Dagli Orti, p. 71; The Granger Collection, New York, p. 83; © Topham/The Image Works, p. 90; The Art Archive/Royal Palace Caserta Italy/Dagli Orti, p. 97; Giraudon/Art Resource, NY, p. 101; © The British Museum/HIP/The Image Works, p. 124; The Art Archive, pp. 134, 135; © Araldo de Luca/CORBIS, p. 143; The Art Archive/Pella Museum Greece/Dagli Orti, p. 144; The Art Archive/Private Collection/Dagli Orti, p. 146.

Cover: © Art Media – Louvre, Paris/Heritage-Images/The Image Works